REBEL WOMEN OF THE GOLD RUSH

Extraordinary Achievements and Daring Adventures

RICH MOLE

VICTORIA · VANCOUVER · CALGARY

Heritage House Publishing Company Ltd.
#108 – 17665 66A Avenue
Surrey, BC V3S 2A7
www.heritagehouse.ca

Heritage House Publishing Company Ltd.
PO Box 468
Custer, WA
98240-0468

Library and Archives Canada Cataloguing in Publication
Mole, Rich, 1946 –
    Rebel women of the gold rush: extraordinary achievements and daring adventures / Rich Mole.

Some parts previously published under title: Rebel women of the Klondike.
Includes bibliographical references.
ISBN 978-1-894974-76-9

    1. Women—Yukon Territory—Klondike River Valley—History. 2. Women—Yukon Territory—Klondike River Valley—Biography. 3. Klondike River Valley (Yukon)—Gold discoveries. I. Title.

FC4022.3.M654 2009   971.9'1   C2008-908136-6

Library of Congress Control Number: 2009920317

Series editor: Lesley Reynolds.
Cover design: Chyla Cardinal. Interior design: Frances Hunter.
Cover photo: "One of the Girls," *circa* 1898, Dawson City Museum (1984.207.5, Eric A. Hegg photographer). Interior photos: Alaska State Library, page 60 (Winter and Pond photographers, PCA-87-682); Glenbow Archives, page 74 (NA-891-5); Yukon Archives, pages 89 and 99 (M.L. Black Collection, 82/218, H-14); National Archives of Canada, page 124 (C-014478); Dawson City Museum, page 136 (984-98-4).

 Mixed Sources
Cert no. SW-COC-001271
© 1996 FSC
FSC

The interior of this book was printed on 100% post-consumer recycled paper, processed chlorine free and printed with vegetable-based inks.

Heritage House acknowledges the financial support for its publishing program from the Government of Canada through the Book Publishing Industry Development Program (BPIDP), Canada Council for the Arts and the province of British Columbia through the British Columbia Arts Council and the Book Publishing Tax Credit.

BRITISH COLUMBIA ARTS COUNCIL
Supported by the Province of British Columbia

The Canada Council | Le Conseil des Arts
for the Arts | du Canada

12 11 10 09   1 2 3 4 5

Printed in Canada

For Shirley, the "Rebel Woman" in my life

Contents

Prologue

MRS. LA GHRIST DECIDED SHE *had heard enough. It had been nearly two years since she had laid eyes on her husband, John La Ghrist. Now, after her new beau had actually paid the lout $1,500 to leave them alone, John was back, begging her to give up her new life in the Klondike and accompany him to Australia. She scoffed. With him? Now? She was doing quite all right, thank you! In Vancouver, on the Stikine Trail and now in Dawson City, she had always made money from "her girls." If John didn't like it, he could go right back to Hamilton, Ontario, where they had come from.*

Suddenly, John demanded something else. He demanded she give him a share of her hard-earned money! She laughed, but when she turned to tell her estranged husband exactly what she thought of him, she was staring into the barrel of his revolver.

Those on the street near the alley entrance heard two shots ring out. They turned to see a woman lurch from the open door of a wooden shack and stagger into the alley. John La Ghrist emerged from the doorway, levelled the revolver at his bleeding wife and fired again. The woman's body jerked with the bullet's impact. She stumbled in the dust of the alley and began crawling away. The onlookers rushed to her aid as John La Ghrist calmly walked back into the shack and slammed the door. As the stunned bystanders turned over the bleeding, semi-conscious woman, they heard another shot from behind the door of the shack.

1

Compelling Motivations

IN A FAR-OFF ALASKA SEAPORT, two steamships slipped their moorings and headed south. On board was a motley collection of passengers who had made the long sternwheeler journey down the Yukon River to St. Michael, on the Bering Sea. Less than a year earlier, these individuals had been as impoverished as the poorest unemployed in Chicago, San Francisco, Winnipeg or Vancouver. Their exhausted demeanour, gaunt, bearded faces and the dishevelled, worn clothing that hung on their bodies still gave them the look of the down-and-out. However, their appearance disguised the fact that by a combination of luck, timing and determination every one of these haggard individuals was now incredibly wealthy. Within days, the personal fortune each had wrested from the frozen ground would bring hope and a sense of purpose to hundreds of thousands of others.

The World They Knew

Historians called the 1890s the Gay Nineties because there was much to be happy about. War was absent from the front pages of the newspapers for the first time in living memory. At last, the civilized world was at peace.

In North America, the anguish of the personal upheaval endured through decades of tumultuous national expansion was a thing of the past. Throughout the continent, the West had been won. In the United States, the Indian Wars were over. In Canada, the North-West Rebellion had been put down just five years earlier. People were enjoying the benefits of transportation systems and communication innovations that triumphed over time and distance. Railways linked tiny inland outposts with metropolises from coast to coast. Fleets of fast clipper ships were setting records as they brought the new world closer to the old. Telegraph wires were humming with messages, and soon telephone wires would be buzzing too.

In urban homes, kitchen taps had replaced iron pumps; flush toilets had replaced outhouses and chamber pots, and electric lights were replacing gas and oil lamps. New, popular music mirrored the bright, lively tempo of the times as pianos were uncrated and rolled into more and more homes. In well-furnished parlours, the sedate triple metre of a familiar Strauss waltz was often augmented by the strident four-four time of a new Sousa march and the fast-tumbling notes of a Scott Joplin "rag."

In the 1890s, North American society was a comforting blend of two worlds: that of men and that of women. This was nothing new. However, those spheres were destined to intersect in ways that the previous generation could not have imagined.

Most women who entered the workplace did so out of dire financial necessity. Usually, women were relegated to mind-numbing factory jobs. The more fortunate, employed as nurses and teachers, regarded their professions as temporary positions. They were expected to abandon work as soon as the right man came along, or certainly as soon as their first "sickness" (pregnancy) overtook them. Those over 40 years of age who were still emptying bedpans or instructing children were doomed to that most unfortunate of all futures—spinsterhood.

Martha Purdy, who spent most of her adult life in the Yukon, recalled her father's attitude toward women. Her 16-year-old mother bore the brunt of it just minutes after giving birth to Martha and her twin sister.

"Susan, I am disappointed," Martha's father frowned. "I expected a boy."

"Yes, I know," Martha's exhausted mother whimpered. "I am so sorry."

At finishing school, Martha studied the usual subjects

then taught to young upper-class women, including elocution and deportment. However, she also successfully mastered "new age" subjects such as calculus and typing. Yet, her father's expectations were those of a typical father of the time. Upon Martha's graduation, a friend asked her father what career he had selected for the "dear girl." Martha always remembered her father's curt reply. "The career of a wife and mother," he snapped.

Located in the frozen wilderness of the Far North, the Klondike was, as the *Seattle Post-Intelligencer*'s headline bluntly stated, NO PLACE FOR WOMEN. "Women are utterly unfit to fight the battle out there," one Klondiker concurred, ignoring the fact that most men were also "utterly unfit," and that didn't stop nearly 30,000 men from setting off from job, home and family in search of Klondike gold. It was enough to stop most women, though. A woman's place was in the home, not on a gold creek.

Perhaps stay-at-home sentiments were best expressed by a *London Times* editor, Flora Shaw, a woman who had visited the gold creeks of the Klondike. In a speech Shaw gave to the Royal Colonial Institute in early 1899, Flora told her mostly male audience, "In the expanse of the Empire, as in other movements, man wins the battle, but woman holds the field." The "field" referred to the household.

What Klondike stampeders needed most, the editor told her audience, was what men everywhere needed. Ignoring the possibility that other women might aspire to her own abilities and achievements, Shaw thought women should stick to what they did best. Their list of objectives should include: "To clean the spot in which they lived—even if it were only a tent or shack—to wash the clothes, to cook the food, to give to one's fireside a human interest." A charitable observer might conclude that Flora Shaw knew her audience well. However, the separate worlds of men and women now seemed to be on a potential collision course.

For the first time, women were on the march for recognition in the workplace, the ability to own property and the right to vote. Surely, most right-thinking men told each other, this path was not one their own wives and daughters would choose to set foot on. Yet the emancipation movement that had begun so tentatively a decade or two before was to be continued more stridently by granddaughters of these protesters, 70 years later.

This was the world Canadian and American women knew, as they and their families and friends celebrated the start of the final tranquil decade in a century of upheaval and hardship. Women were poised to enjoy a gentler, better, "happier" world than their mothers and grandmothers had ever known. But just when expectations were highest, dark clouds of discontent and despair were gathering on the sunny horizon of the 20th century.

Desperate Times
On November 11, 1890, Henry Swift, the general manager

of Nova Scotia's huge Springhill Mines operation, was a worried man. The mine conditions were dark and dangerous. Pit boys working for a pittance were forever beset with bruises and broken bones. Workers faced threatening water levels, rotting timbers and pockets of poison gas. A miner's lot had not changed much in a century.

"I am doing all I can to keep things straight and can do no more," Henry wrote to his boss. It was, he added, "enough worry to kill a man." Mere worry didn't kill Henry Swift. The day after he wrote that letter, a mine shaft was rocked by a fiery blast. That explosion ended Henry's life, as well as those of 124 other beloved husbands and sons. Canada's worst mining disaster was an ominous portent of things to come.

A little more than a year later, at Homestead, Pennsylvania, disgruntled Carnegie Mill steelworkers took off their gloves, dropped their shovels and walked off the job. Hired enforcers attempted to coerce the men back to work. Families grieved as 18 men died in the street-fighting carnage that followed.

In 1893, shortly after ringing in the new year, an unheard-of event occurred: the Philadelphia and Reading Railroad went bankrupt. Banks and their mortgage-company cousins began to close their doors, shutting out tens of thousands of stunned depositors and lenders. Savings and investments vanished. Before the year staggered to its conclusion, three other major American railroads had parked their locomotives and dismissed thousands of employees.

By this time, one-sixth of the American work force—

four million angry, desperate men and women—were unemployed. Staring into empty wallets, people all over North America simply stopped spending. Scores of retail outlets closed their doors in response.

Economic conditions were bleakest in the Pacific Northwest. At low tide, many began to walk exposed sandy beaches to dig up clams for the kitchen table. Unaccustomed to the humiliation of rejection, men grew despondent. In turn, their wives guiltily endured their frustrated husbands' anger and the whines of hungry ragtag children. The descendants of one such Washington State family never forgot those tough times.

John and Emma Feero had five children. Family size was a source of pride to Feero, as long as his Tacoma transportation company was profitable. The railroad closures hit hard, causing Feero to lose everything but two horses and a wagon. Clamouring to be fed, his large family became a crushing responsibility. As John relentlessly searched for work, Emma scrimped and made do. The family was forced to relocate five times in four years.

The Godsend from the North
In the summer of 1897, two coastal steamers disgorged their precious Klondike cargoes in San Francisco and Seattle. The arrival of the ships triggered the last and greatest gold rush in history.

GOLD! GOLD! GOLD! GOLD! screamed the headline of

the *Seattle Post-Intelligencer* on Saturday, July 17, 1897. In a depressed port city full of desperate people, gold meant the end of hardship and want. Gold was something few people had, nearly everybody dreamed about and many would do anything to get. For 68 rich arrivals on the steamship *Portland*, and dozens more who had hefted their bullion off the *Excelsior* in San Francisco two days earlier, that dream had come true. They had found what everybody wanted—bags, boxes and rawhide bundles of gold—and had brought it back home to tempt the rest of the world. The two ships had brought in two million dollars worth of temptation, the *San Francisco Chronicle* reported. More than a century later, this amount still signifies wealth. At a time when a 50-cent piece bought a full-course dinner at a respectable restaurant, the sum was almost unimaginable.

GOING TO SCOOP UP THE GOLD, trumpeted the *San Francisco Call* five days after the *Portland*'s headline-making arrival. That day, the overloaded steamer was churning the water of the Puget Sound, on its way back up the coast once again. The decks were crammed; every stateroom was taken. Among the hundreds squeezed on board those first overbooked boats was John Feero. Emma had agreed to stay home with the kids while he went north to strike it rich.

Nearly one year later, the North-West Mounted Police (NWMP) estimated 19,000 would-be prospectors had passed through customs posts on their journey over the mountains and down the Yukon River to Dawson City. Fewer than 700 of these hopefuls—a meagre 3.5 percent—were women. But in an era when most men did whatever they wanted and many women found they could not, it is astonishing that the gold-hungry hordes included any women at all.

Blissful Ignorance

News of enormous gold discoveries flashed by telegram up the coast and to the east after the *Excelsior* tied up in San Francisco that Thursday. The ship had taken the California port city by surprise. When the *Portland* edged against the wharf's timbers in Seattle two days later, thousands were waiting on the waterfront, eager to witness the parade of new millionaires staggering down the gangway and heaving their riches aboard waiting wagons. Gold fever was about to hit its zenith, infecting tens of thousands of men—and many women, as well. One of them was Wild West show performer Mae McKamish Meadows, who had been living in Santa Cruz, California.

"The people have gold sacked up like wheat lying all around," the excited woman wrote to relatives back home when she and her sharpshooter husband, Charley, hit Juneau, Alaska. Mae hadn't actually seen the gold (she was quoting a letter from faraway Dawson City), but, she enthused, the reports "would make you want to have a flying machine and go at once!" Mae's hopes were high. "If we can only get in we will be ready to come back next summer and buy out Santa Cruz!"

In Chicago, Emily Craig and her husband of 10 years were leading a quiet, comfortable life when the Klondike strikes made headlines. The Craigs were thrilled by the newspaper stories. Not long afterward, Emily's husband confessed to her that he had actually seen some Klondike nuggets in a jeweller's store display. The very next day, Emily stood with her nose pressed to the store window, gazing at the gold on the other side of the glass, as enraptured as her husband had been. "From then on, I could believe any story," she admitted. "We both caught gold fever—and that is no childhood disease, either." The Craigs were soon on their way across the country.

Not all women who said goodbye to friends and family to make the trek to the Yukon were naive. Ethel Berry, who left a full year ahead of the mob with her new husband, Clarence, knew a little of what lay ahead. "I was prepared for the hardships, having known perfectly well before I decided to go that it would be no bed of roses," Ethel said. Ethel had the advantage of insider information: Clarence had already been prospecting in the Yukon for two years.

In early 1898, New Yorker Marie Riedeselle decided to join the rush. However, before she boarded her ship, the former Connecticut farmer undertook a three-month strategic plan to learn as much as she could about the place. This exercise was so unusual (most men did no planning), that Marie's efforts caught the attention of the *Seattle Daily Times*.

Marie "knows accurately the geography of the country,

knows the customs and habits of the people there, the kind of garments best adapted to the climate," the newspaper reported. Marie's unseemly behaviour intensified as she attempted to master the physical skills she thought she would need, including "how to handle dogs, manage a loaded sled, propel a boat; in fact how to do everything a human being needs to do in that country." These skills took strength and stamina. The former masseuse undertook a daily physical workout with the same zeal as she conducted her research, and the reporter assured his bemused readers, "Her muscles are in perfect condition for her great undertaking."

Ethel and Marie were exceptions. For most, ignorance was bliss. Why spoil the fun? It was all so easy—just buy a ticket, pack your clothes and "Ho, for the Klondike!" "Women have made up their minds to go to the Klondike, so there is no use trying to discourage them . . . our wills are strong and courage unfailing," a woman reporter told readers of *The Skagway News*.

Soon, however, hundreds of women would learn that strong wills and unfailing courage would scarcely be enough. Their lessons would come quickly—and painfully.

2

Nothing to Lose

FOR ANY MEMBER OF THE "weaker sex" to join the gold-rush adventure appeared to be folly and madness. The Yukon terrain was so hostile and living conditions so horrific that the experience quickly drove the strongest men to insanity and sometimes suicide. Like men, women of the Klondike often risked everything. What would compel women to endure discomfort and danger, including frostbite and freezing, flash flood, fire and avalanche? Why would women risk the ravages of scurvy, tuberculosis, pneumonia, meningitis and typhoid—diseases that wrecked or shortened the lives of thousands of Klondikers? For most men, and some women, too, the obvious answer was gold—the chance to strike it rich. For others, the answers were far more complex.

Sensing an Opportunity

Belinda Mulrooney stood in shock and dismay. Across the busy San Francisco street, the firemen had done their best, but it was too little, too late. Belinda watched as the building that housed her newly sublet restaurant continued to smoulder. For weeks, she had poured time, effort and money into the dilapidated structure. Her new West Coast real-estate venture had eaten up most of the $8,000 profit from the sale of her Chicago World's Fair restaurant. Now, all of that capital had just gone up in smoke.

The fire was a disastrous setback for the young woman who had enjoyed a rags-to-riches experience since coming to America as an impoverished Irish teenager. Years before, her parents had fled the Emerald Isle in search of a better life, leaving their little girl behind. When she was just 13, Belinda set sail to join her family in the United States. Reuniting with her estranged family in Archibald, Pennsylvania, was not a happy occasion. Belinda didn't like dirt, the coal dust of the Pennsylvania mines or her dirt-poor Irish family. Within weeks of their ill-fated reunion, Belinda became obsessed with one thought: she must make enough money to leave. Her mother, Maria, was not pleased when Belinda left for the biggest city in the state, Philadelphia. "You are the queerest human being I ever saw in my life," Maria Mulrooney told her wilful daughter. "I don't understand you."

Once in Philadelphia, it wasn't long before Belinda was

hired as a nanny by a wealthy couple. It was a dream come true. Unlike Belinda's father, George King Cummings and his wife, Belle, did not awaken at 4 a.m. to crawl down a coal mine. The Cummings taught Belinda many lessons.

"What's this?" Belinda asked Belle. Her paycheque, Belle explained. Belinda handed it back. "Save it for me." Belinda had never been in a bank. Belle took her there to establish a savings account.

The teenaged nanny began to formulate ideas about life. She wanted a house like the Cummings had, to dress the way they dressed, to speak the way they spoke and to have money. She believed the secret to obtaining these luxuries was to become an entrepreneur.

Soon, Belinda was reading newspaper stories about factory shutdowns. Mr. Cummings was worried. Belinda listened carefully when her employer explained about the financial crash. Belinda then offered to lend the family her entire $600 bank account. Times were difficult, Belle Cummings laughed, but not that difficult.

Belinda knew better. She could wait and worry, or take matters into her own hands. After a casual visit with the cook and the housemaid next door, Belinda decided to take action. The three women opened a restaurant in Chicago, where the 1890s version of the world's fair, the "World's Columbian Exposition," was being built, complete with canals, a lagoon, graceful iron and glass buildings and a new invention called the Ferris wheel. However, it wasn't long before Belinda sensed a new opportunity in California. She sold the restaurant and headed west.

Now, with her San Francisco property a smoking ruin and most of her Chicago fair proceeds gone, Belinda decided to search for job prospects on the waterfront.

"What can you do?" Thomas R. Turner snapped. As Pacific Coast Steamships' port steward, Turner had no time for a young woman looking for a job, when so many men were out of work.

"I don't know," Belinda admitted. "Tell me what I have to do and I will do the best I can."

Turner looked at the woman in front of him more closely. She was short but well built, and she had unflinching, calculating eyes behind steel-rimmed spectacles. "Well, what do you want to do?" he asked.

Belinda remembered seeing posters advertising passage to a new and exciting destination. "I want to work on one of the ships going to Alaska."

"Out of the question," Turner replied. "They don't carry stewardesses." Then Turner remembered a note from the *Santa Rosa*, one of two ships on the San Diego run, saying a stewardess had fallen sick. Turner made Belinda an offer. She accepted.

A few weeks later, Belinda was knocking on Turner's office door again. "Thanks, Mr. Turner, but I'm looking for something else. Too many whiny women on that run."

Turner couldn't ignore the *Santa Rosa*'s reports describing how hard the feisty little woman had worked. "Okay, Miss Mulrooney," he replied. Perhaps she was more comfortable with rough-and-ready men. "I'll try you on the Alaska run."

Three years later, Belinda's desperate flight from poverty would lead her to Dawson City, Yukon. There, mining figured prominently in her life once again, but she wouldn't work on her hands and knees as her father had done. Instead, she would stand tall as a mine owner and broker who bought and sold other people's mines. The girl who had nothing to lose in Pennsylvania found she had everything to gain in the Klondike. But Belinda Mulrooney was not alone.

Nellie Cashman had an important decision to make. Like Belinda Mulrooney, the Irish teenager had set sail for America full of hope for a better life. Nellie found it in an unlikely, unladylike setting: a raw, raucous gold camp in 1870s Nevada. The only woman in the place, and still unmarried, Nellie somehow retained her virtue and earned the admiration of the men. When not actively prospecting, she ran a boarding house. As gold and silver petered out, Nellie, determined and adventurous, decided to tag along with hundreds of prospectors who were making their way to BC's remote Cassiar gold fields.

Cashman loved her footloose lifestyle and followed her fortunes to California, New Mexico, Colorado and Arizona. She was running a store, hotel and restaurant in Tombstone when the Earps and Doc Holliday had their deadly date with the Clantons at the OK Corral. She left the American West for prospecting hot spots in Mexico and South Africa. When the call of the Klondike echoed around the world, her way of life was already established. Although regarded as a woman of advanced years— she was almost 50—Nellie still had plenty of energy. She quickly organized an Alaska gold-mining company. Nellie thought she had nothing to lose and everything to gain by heading off to the Yukon. There, in addition to being recognized as a successful prospector, she earned a lasting reputation as an adventurous entrepreneur.

While Nellie Cashman was buying her train ticket for the West Coast, Marguerite Laimee was booking passage on a ship. She was leaving the gold camps of Australia on the first leg of her long journey to the Yukon. Having married at 14 and divorced at 16, Marguerite would never gain favour in polite society. Instead, she set off to follow the prospectors to far-flung locales, where her unorthodox behaviour was tolerated, if not encouraged.

Alone and anxious to make another new start, Marguerite arrived in Dawson City at the height of the rush in July 1898. She prospered in the bustling little riverside shantytown. However, Marguerite's greatest acquisition wasn't gold, real estate or her profitable—but somewhat morally suspect— cigar-store business. Her greatest happiness came from marriage to the man who was arguably the Klondike stampede's most important individual.

Seeing the World

Kate Ryan's heart had been broken. Statuesque, buxom and 22 years old, the six-foot-tall farmer's daughter from Johnsville, New Brunswick, had eyes only for Simon Gallagher. Alas, Simon was the son of a prosperous family and had a very status-conscious mother. To head off what Mrs. Gallagher thought was a disastrous match, she convinced her good Catholic son to enter the seminary. She thought it better to be in the priesthood than to marry below your social position. Simon had the good grace to break the news to Kate himself. His studies meant he would soon be leaving the area, he told her.

"I'm leaving, too," Kate blurted. Now a rejected, single woman, Kate realized there was nothing left for her in the New Brunswick hamlet where she had been raised. Her mother agreed.

"Go, Kate," Anne Ryan urged as her daughter hesitated to board the train. "Here is your chance to see the world."

By September 1893, Kate was working in Seattle as her mother's cousin's housekeeper and nanny. Two years later, she was training as a hospital worker. Back in Canada, and on her way to work at Vancouver's St. Paul's Hospital one sunny July day, Kate heard *Sun* newsboys shouting out the newspaper's stunning headline: GOLD IN THE YUKON!

Kate's imagination ignited. She was single, free of responsibility and had saved a little money. Before the end of the year, Kate was inside the city's Hudson's Bay store, ordering supplies for her trip north. On February 28, 1898, Kate and her five grey huskies were standing on the deck of the steamer *Tees*, watching the city slip away as they headed out of Seymour Narrows. It was the beginning of a year-long journey to the Klondike and a life she had known only in her dreams.

Playing the Odds

Faith Fenton, the esteemed editor of *Canadian Home Journal*, had just been fired. When the publishers showed Faith the door, it wasn't because of lack of ability. It was politics, pure and simple. Despite a growing chorus of objections, Faith continued to support the wife of the new Governor General, Lady Ishbel Aberdeen, who insisted on advancing women's rights. It was the wrong thing to do in conservative Toronto.

The dismissal was a bitter professional blow to Canada's first female magazine editor and former Toronto reporter and columnist. Her name had become trusted by tens of thousands of Canadian and US magazine and newspaper readers. Eleven years earlier, as schoolteacher Alice Freeman, Faith had convinced Barrie, Ontario's *Northern Advance* to publish her slice-of-life series on lighthouse keepers and their families. Alice then succeeded in signing on at the *Toronto Globe* under the byline "Faith Fenton." All the while, she continued her "real job" as a schoolteacher.

Old-age homes, women's prisons, orphanages and hospitals were Fenton's beat as she researched her popular social-issue stories. She paid the price for her passion and confessed her doubt in a column: "A woman's bitterest moment, I think—especially if she be a woman unloved and therefore lonely—is when she turns from the mirror realizing for the first time that the fair flush of youth has vanished."

Now, she had lost her job. The firing was a personal blow, as well as a professional setback. Three years earlier, Faith had finally given up teaching and taken the plunge as a full-time reporter. Now, Faith was 40 and living on skimpy freelance fees. She had nothing to lose by heading north. Happily, the *Globe* thought so too and made her their gold-rush correspondent. Things were looking better already.

3

Seekers and Runaways

IT WASN'T ALWAYS THE LURE of gold or the chance to earn a bigger income that goaded many women northward through the Alaskan mountain passes to the long, winding Yukon River. Others were seeking something else—aid for loved ones, a husband, an opportunity to grow and learn or simply an adventure.

The Seekers

In certain cases, the special something Klondike adventurers sought was in fact a special someone. Just before she was fired from her job as magazine editor, Faith Fenton had the good fortune to interview Canada's minister of the interior, William Ogilvie. Ten years earlier, while working as a surveyor, Ogilvie had spent time in the Klondike, plotting the boundary between the Yukon and Alaska. Ogilvie privately assured Faith that marriage prospects were excellent in the Yukon. That was an understatement. In the Klondike in 1898, men outnumbered women by at least 13 to 1. Seven months after she stepped off the boat at Wrangell, Alaska, Faith succeeded in ending the "unloved and therefore lonely" existence she had once confessed to her readers.

When Faith finally reached Dawson City in September 1898, five months after leaving Ottawa, her arrival was big news. The *Klondike Nugget* hailed the presence of "a brilliant Canadian writer of magazine and newspaper fame." With such a public introduction, Faith was perhaps fated to find her man, but it was the man who found her.

Years later, her future husband was able to recall the first day he had glimpsed the gaunt, exhausted tent-dweller walking along the Yukon River. It is likely it was love at first sight. Her observer was Dr. John Nelson Elliot Brown, head secretary to William Ogilvie, who, since meeting Faith in Ottawa, had returned to the Yukon as commissioner of the territory. Brown was the territory's medical health officer and a member of the Yukon Council. Within two weeks of sighting Faith on the riverbank, Brown offered her a position as Ogilvie's assistant private secretary. This favoured vantage point gave the part-time reporter an insider's understanding of what-was-what and who-was-who in Dawson and the Klondike.

The Fenton-Brown marriage on January 1, 1900, was a

fitting start to the new year's social whirl. The couple entertained often, with Martha Purdy among their acquaintances. They lived in Dawson until 1905, when Brown accepted a position at Toronto General Hospital. Soon, Dr. John Brown's byline—he'd dreamed of becoming a writer—was seen far more often than Faith's, as she became the supportive wife of a senior medical administrator and a lady of leisure.

Faith was just one of dozens of marriage-minded women who packed up for the Yukon. On the scent of a story, a *San Francisco Examiner* reporter faked a classified ad, claiming to be an anonymous prospector headed for the Yukon. The man invited a matrimonially inclined young lady or widow to accompany him. The enterprising journalist received more than 30 responses.

"I could be a helpmate to you," replied an 18-year-old husband-seeker whose family was all deceased, "and the union would be an advantage to me, for I find it a hard struggle in this world, without relatives."

"I don't look for perfection in any man; we all have our faults," one 28-year-old widow added solicitously. "I am willing to chance it—you, marriage, Alaska and all."

One practical New York woman decided to assess her odds of gold-rush matrimony without the discomfort and expense of travelling across the continent. She sent the text of a want ad on the back of a photograph of herself to the Dawson City's *Klondike Nugget*. She didn't want to apply for a job, she wrote publisher Gene Allen, she wanted "to apply for a rich husband."

The photo "is of a pretty young girl of about 20 years of age," Allen told his readers. "Now then you Hunker [Creek] Princes and Eldorado Kings," he urged, "come and see the photo, see the letter, get the address and pay for the ad."

* * *

Five years before gold fever infected the world, veteran Alaska trader John Healy and his wife stepped off the train in Chicago. The couple had travelled thousands of kilometres from the far-off Yukon River gold hamlet of Fortymile. Healy wasn't there for a holiday; he had come for one reason only: to raise money. Inside an office building, he met an old Montana fur-trading associate, Portus B. Weare. Healy laid out his ideas for a Yukon River transportation company. There was much more gold to be found, he told his friend. Healy was sure men all over the US would be desperate for ways to get their hands on the gold. Weare invited the Healys to his fashionable home for dinner.

Bridget Mannion worked as a cook for Portus Weare and his family. She was in the kitchen when Healy regaled the Weares with exciting and colourful stories of his adventures at his isolated trading post at Dyea, just a few miles north of the future gold-rush town of Skagway. The family listened in fascination to Healy's plans for the transportation company and a new trading post situated where the Yukon River met the Fortymile River. Bridget was behind the kitchen door when she first heard the words "Alaska" and "Yukon." The words and the stories around them fired her imagination. Before long, the cook approached the master of the house and told him bluntly that she was off to Fortymile.

"But you can't mine," sneered the incredulous Weare.

"That's true," Mannion admitted, "but there's them that can."

Weare's cook had no intention of mining. She had arranged for Belle and John Healy to hire her as a domestic. Bridget was after a husband, some lucky prospector who would simply dig nuggets out of the ground for her.

More than a year later, a fashionable young woman strode into Portus Weare's office. When he looked up, Weare's jaw dropped. Then he took the elegantly gloved hand extended by his former cook. The name wasn't Mannion any more, Bridget informed him. At Fortymile's first wedding ceremony, Bridget had become Mrs. Frank Aylward. The wealthy couple was off to Ireland to visit her family, and she had just stopped by to say hello. "Before I got fifty miles up the Yukon, I had received 125 proposals of marriage," she informed the astonished and delighted Weare. She held off, though, she said, until she met "an engaging compatriot with a Kerry brogue and [a] mine that panned at the rate of $50,000 a month."

* * *

For Frances Dorley, a 26-year-old Seattle milliner and dressmaker who lived with her parents, life had become dull and uninteresting. With the arrival of the *Portland*, the city's residents had gone crazy. It must have seemed to Frances' worried parents that she had gone crazy, too. Frances might not have used the word "adventure," but that was clearly what the sheltered woman was seeking when she told her mother and father she was leaving her predictable life behind and would be travelling north.

Mr. and Mrs. Dorley opposed her rash plan. The fact that Frances was not travelling alone did not lessen their concern. Instead, when they realized that their daughter's travelling companions were three men, and that Frances had agreed to cook for them, their fears likely increased exponentially. Eventually, they reached a compromise. The old folks finally agreed to give their blessing, but only on the condition that Frances must return to her Seattle home (and therefore her senses) in three weeks' time. Frances quickly agreed.

Frances kept her part of the deal, but it was a fool's bargain. When she got a taste of the madness in Skagway, Alaska, the port-of-call for thousands of eager prospectors who were about to hike their way to the Klondike, she was a goner. Once home, she had barely unpacked before she began pestering her parents about travelling to Dawson.

Frances later conceded that her parents' concerns were justified. Nevertheless, she wrote, "after three weeks of insistent pleading, I finally won my mother's tearful consent and my father's reluctant blessing." She sailed again for Alaska the following April. After almost four months of travelling, she eventually reached Dawson at the height of gold-rush activity and loved the "muddy, gold-crazy settlement of shacks and tents."

The following year, Frances found even more to love. During Christmas celebrations in 1899, she bit down hard on a hazelnut and chipped her tooth. By now, Dawson City boasted modern city conveniences, including dental services, and she found herself in the office of Dr. Alexander Gillis, who had arrived in Dawson around the same time as Frances. First, he cemented the tooth of his newest patient, and then, possessed of an outgoing and disarming disposition, began cementing a serious relationship with her.

Alex and Frances married in 1902. The couple enjoyed hobnobbing with Dawson's "movers and shakers," Alex helping to establish a Masonic Lodge and Frances becoming first officer in the women's auxiliary, Daughters of the Eastern Star. The Gillises made the Klondike their home for 20 years.

* * *

About the time young Frances Dorley was saying goodbye to her parents in Seattle, San Francisco mother Georgia Hacker White was raising her children alone, in an era when being a separated mother carried a particularly painful social stigma. The unrelenting needs of three young children kept Georgia housebound and nearly destitute. The Klondike Gold Rush seemed a unique opportunity. Georgia reluctantly made arrangements for her children to stay with friends in

Nevada and with the Ladies Protective Relief Society in San Francisco. Then she boarded the *Australia*.

Georgia's guilt and despair plagued her continuously. On the first exhausting leg of her journey to Dawson City, she poured out her anguish in her diary. "I think constantly of my little ones and God knows at times it seems more than I can bear but I must—for Oh, deliver me from becoming insane up here." Georgia somehow found the strength to continue on, albeit briefly. Two months later, she was back in San Francisco, no wealthier than when she had left. However, the experience seemed to stiffen her resolve. She reclaimed her children and divorced her husband.

Georgia never did find financial fortune, but during that first voyage north on the *Australia*, she found something far more valuable—the love of a fellow passenger named Frank Mills. Georgia and Frank were married in 1902.

* * *

Anna DeGraf was a seeker of a different sort. An economic panic in the 1870s left Anna and her husband penniless in New York. Anna stayed with their son and daughter while her husband went prospecting in Washington State. When she went to join him, Anna discovered that her husband had been murdered. The widowed mother somehow managed to start a dressmaking business in Seattle. Unfortunately, she suffered the fate of many business owners of the time; everything she owned was destroyed by fire. Then her son disappeared.

"Goodbye, Mother. I'll see you in 14 days," George told Anna as she waved to him from the front steps of her Seattle home. Her boy was off on an Alaskan adventure. "I'll see you in 14 days," he shouted back to her as he strode down the street. They were the last words Anna DeGraf ever heard him speak.

At the time of her son's disappearance, Anna was 53. Instead of resigning herself to fast-approaching old age, Anna sold her business, packed up her sewing machine and headed north to look for her missing son. She arrived in Juneau and received a report that others had seen George in the city. Then Joe Ladue, a trader and future millionaire who would soon establish Dawson City, told her George and others had stopped at his trading post at Ogilvie, on the Yukon River. So in 1894, three years before the rush, Anna made her way to the Klondike. Four years later, Anna's search had proved fruitless.

Anna had returned to San Francisco and was living near her daughter when gold-rush excitement reached its zenith. Anna, now 59, made the arduous trek north once again. She was hoping against hope that gold fever had infected her long-lost son and that she would find him in Dawson City. Decades passed, and Anna DeGraf never did find her missing son. What she found instead was the captivating lure of the North, a lure that pulled her back again and again to live a life full of memorable adventures.

* * *

Many who ventured north simply sought to help others.

Among them was a group of four women representing a brand new medical aid organization, the Victorian Order of Nurses (VON). The brainchild of controversial Canadian social activist Lady Ishbel Aberdeen, the VON was initiated in honour of Queen Victoria's Diamond Jubilee. Concerned as much for their own reputations as they were for the welfare of their patients, doctors raised predictable howls of protest at Lady Aberdeen's unseemly concept. Nevertheless, the organization accepted its first recruits in the fall of 1897, just a few months before the gold rush afforded the VON's Klondike contingent a supreme test of fortitude.

Sending nurses to the Klondike was a shrewd decision on Lady Aberdeen's part. Who could protest against women who were willing to make incredible sacrifices to care for fathers, sons and brothers in the northern wilderness? No pompous doctor could compete with that kind of public relations. The nurses' departure, celebrated with a glittering farewell dinner at the Governor General's residence, proved a wonderful opportunity to further the VON's cause.

As the train rolled out of Ottawa on its way to Vancouver, the four nurses had the pleasure of sharing their private car with *Globe* correspondent Faith Fenton, who would help ensure that the VON continued to enjoy good press. The women had more company when they boarded the *Islander* in Vancouver: they were joined by the newly assembled Yukon Field Force, a military unit of close to 200 men sent to bolster the overwhelmed NWMP contingent.

Although it might have been a happy coincidence that
the Yukon Field Force was on the trail at the same time as
the nurses, Ishbel Aberdeen recognized this stroke of luck
and was quick to strike a bargain: military protection for
her angels of mercy in exchange for medical assistance for
the unit's 190 or more officers and men. While two nurses
remained at the unit's Fort Selkirk headquarters on the upper
Yukon River, two others continued on to Dawson City's
recently opened Good Samaritan Presbyterian Hospital.

The VON's work began on the trail as they ministered
to military men and the civilians they met along the way.
It was a mild prelude to the horrors that lay ahead. With
no sanitary system to serve its 18,000 residents, and little
fresh food to feed them, Dawson was one of the unhealthiest
places in North America. The city's two hospitals were
quickly filled to capacity with people suffering from scurvy,
typhoid, venereal disease—the list went on and on.

"I thought I had seen something of typhoid fever, but
nothing like this," nurse Georgia Powell wrote to Lady
Aberdeen. "Of severe haemorrhage cases, we had six at one
time. Typhoid with pneumonia, with malaria, congestion
of the liver, rheumatism, neuralgia, sore throat, discharge
from the ears and sore eyes. Such sick men! Nor was the
sickness all, but the filth and the vermin . . . Often a patient
lay for days with only a blanket between him and the boards,
thankful if we could give him a sack of shavings."

With symptoms that included bruised, discoloured

flesh, suppurating sores and bleeding gums, scurvy was a particularly unpleasant scourge, not only for its malnourished victims, but also for the women treating them as well. "Disgusting work," Georgia confessed to Lady Aberdeen. "The scrubbing and cleaning of these miserable creatures— and how some would fight against the bath!"

Accommodations for the two nurses in Dawson City were far worse than those of their hospital patients. The women endured freezing temperatures while living in a small tent nearby. Not surprisingly, one of the nurses took ill, and she was forced to undergo surgery in the log hospital's primitive operating theatre. At the Grand Forks hospital, Georgia's nursing colleague Margaret Payson lived inside the hospital, but her "room" was merely a corner of the ward curtained off from her patients. She was forced to sleep on the cold, wooden floor.

It is a credit to the unstinting efforts of these women that suffering was eased, men recovered and as Georgia Powell told Aberdeen proudly, "Not one of these patients had a bed sore or even a chafe, so closely were they watched and attended."

In another illustration of self-sacrifice, an American woman named Lillian Oliver was intrigued by her friend's plan to venture to the Yukon. Lillian's husband was a sick man. She was desperate to make enough money to allow him to quit working. If her friend could chance a trip to the Yukon, perhaps she could too. "I saw in my mind's eye the vision of a proud wife bearing home to a long-suffering man the wherewithal to take him away from dreary toil and give his tired brain a rest," she imagined. "I was watching for the colour to come back to cheeks that had long been a stranger to it; I saw fire come to the eye grown dim; elasticity to steps grown weak; and happiness to both of us."

The Olivers' parting was heart-wrenching. The ailing husband asked God to keep his wife safe. He made Lillian promise that regardless of her success, she would return after no more than two years.

* * *

Martha Purdy, now a young Chicago socialite wife, was very intrigued. The ruby eyes of an ornate, golden metal serpent seemed to move across her palm. Peering closely at her right hand, the great Indian palmist Cheiro intoned somewhat ominously, "You are leaving the country within the year. You will travel far. You will face danger, privation and sorrow." Martha smiled and stifled a mocking laugh. The young, happily married woman had every reason to think the palmist's predictions were altogether too outrageous.

Despite railroad strikes that exasperated and worried her father, Martha's economic future was secure. She had married handsome Will Purdy, son of the president of the Rock Island Railway. The vast fortunes of both families insulated the young couple from any personal suffering. Even after the birth of her two sons, Martha's affluent, leisurely lifestyle continued much as before. She attended an endless round of concerts and plays, volunteered at the children's kindergarten, participated in outings with the cycling club (the bicycle built for two was all the rage) and played games of euchre with the ladies after enjoying afternoon teas prepared by the Purdys' "coloured" servant girl.

The wealthy families' support of the Chicago World's Fair brought Martha into contact with an international who's who. She was chosen to be an attendant of Lady Ishbel Aberdeen. The Governor General's wife had raised funds for the fair's Irish Building and travelled from Canada for its opening. There, Martha also met one of Lady Aberdeen's companions, reporter Faith Fenton. Perhaps it was after meeting these dynamic women that Martha came to a realization: although she had every reason to be happy, something was missing from her life. Simply put, she was bored.

One day, Will Purdy came home full of plans to join the gold rush with a friend, Eli Gage. Martha's pulse quickened as she listened to Will's ideas. Eli, a banker's son who had just returned from Alaska, was married to a woman who had gold-rush connections. One of the two sternwheelers that had taken the newly rich prospectors to "the outside" just a few months earlier was named for Eli's brother-in-law, Chicago businessman and investor Portus B. Weare.

Will and Eli planned to profit from their gold-rush venture before they even left the windy city. They quickly purchased two ocean-going tugs, a steamer and two sailing ships, vessels desperately needed to take gold-crazed hopefuls to the Pacific coast. Martha and Eli's wife started packing.

Once they reached the Yukon, Martha would be no idle spectator. Her mission was to locate the claim of a long-lost uncle of a Rock Island employee. The old prospector had willed his family the million-dollar proceeds from his Klondike claim. The employee entrusted the will itself to Martha, with the promise to pay her 50 percent of the proceeds once she had discovered the location of the golden legacy.

As soon as Martha climbed into the Pullman car for the train trip west, the Indian palmist's prediction about travels became reality. Martha might have paused to wonder about other things Cheiro had mentioned: "danger, privation, sorrow." Perhaps she pondered the Indian's final prediction: "You will have another child."

In Seattle, as the group prepared to board their steamer to Alaska, Will suddenly informed Martha that he had changed his plans: he was off to the Sandwich Islands (modern-day Hawaii). Martha was stunned. Will calmly waited for her to nod in agreement. Where husbands went, wives followed. Instead, it was his turn to be shocked. Incensed at his callous attitude, Martha told her husband he could go where he wanted, but she was off to the Klondike. Martha never saw Will Purdy again. It would be more than a year before she would be reunited with her two boys.

Running Away

The Klondike was the perfect destination for runaways who

wanted anonymity. Virtually everyone was a stranger, mail delivery was sporadic, and telegraph wires had yet to be strung. In the Klondike, the embarrassments, threats and dangers of a previous life remained a secret.

Along with 150 matrimonial hopefuls who had booked passage from New York on the *City of Columbia* was a woman who had absolutely no interest in finding a male companion. In fact, the woman who called herself Nettie Hoven had booked passage simply to escape one. Nettie's live-in New York lover, John Mellen, was a dangerous man. He had threatened to kill her. So, the woman the *Klondike Nugget* later described as "full of pluck and determination" made up her mind to disappear. It wasn't an easy task.

Nettie (most likely a false identity) was not a paying passenger. She worked as a ship's stewardess in exchange for passage around Cape Horn to Seattle. In the Straits of Magellan, the ship went aground. "For three days and three nights we remained upon a rocky island in the vicinity of a cannibal village," the shipwreck victim told an awestruck *Nugget* reporter once she finally reached Dawson City. "The natives were nearly seven feet high and very savage and we were constantly in fear of an attack." Fortunately, crew members patched the vessel, and the ship was able to round Cape Horn. They stopped again at Valparaiso for more extensive repairs, which were made at the expense of the near-destitute passengers. When the ship finally limped into Seattle, most of its passengers were forced to end their travels. They had run out of money. That didn't stop Nettie. She was determined to leave her old life behind.

As she strolled along the Seattle waterfront, Nettie saw a ship readying itself for a trip to St. Michael, Alaska. Bag in hand, she walked up the gangway and boarded the ship. Nobody noticed Nettie until the vessel had left the dock. Unable to put her ashore, the captain put her to work. By the time she reached Dawson City, Nettie had been travelling for seven months and "it didn't cost her a cent," the *Nugget* reported. Nettie stated that she managed to "reach Dawson with money in my pocket, so I think I aught to be satisfied."

Nettie might have been satisfied, but she was not safe. Her vengeful lover was still on her trail. Once John Mellon arrived on the Yukon River, only the threat of action by the NWMP and formal court documents could put the obsessed man in his place (which, authorities warned him, was anywhere but the Yukon) and finally bring Nettie peace of mind.

Whether they were motivated by the boredom of affluence, the agony of abject poverty, a shady past, the quest for adventure or the desire to find gold—or a man who dug it up—in a sense, all of the women who journeyed to the Yukon River were runaways. Each seized the once-in-a-lifetime opportunity of the Klondike Gold Rush, but few had any idea just how far they would run to reach their destination, nor could they have imagined the horrors they would face on their journey.

4

Routes to
the Riches

AS THEY BEGAN THEIR JOURNEY to the Yukon, many women had only the vaguest idea how they would reach their Klondike destination. Often, travellers only learned at the last minute that there were several routes to the riches. They might have wondered which route was the best, but the more important question, if only they had known to ask it, would have been, "Which route is less horrific than the others?"

The All-American Routes
Those who chose to travel via American routes to the Klondike attempted to reach the interior gold fields from the head of Cook Inlet, where Anchorage, Alaska, is located today. They would journey just below the inlet, through Prince William

Sound at Valdez, or farther south over the coastal Malaspina Glacier. Americans chose these routes to avoid paying duties to Canadian customs. Few realized that by choosing these money-saving routes, they stood an excellent chance of losing their health, sanity and even their lives.

Few of the 3,500 men and women who attempted to reach Dawson from the southern Alaska port of Valdez succeeded. In February 1898, the weather along this all-American route was so terrible that frightened, sickened animals, including horses and dogs, had to be shot. Hundreds of stampeders were forced to pull heavy sleds as they trudged through snow, sleet and rain and slid over treacherous ice. After nine exhausting kilometres, they had only just reached the edge of the towering Valdez Glacier that stood between them and the Yukon. By August, when the ice and snow melted, the glacier was impassable. Travellers became snow-blind, collapsed from scurvy and went quietly—or not so quietly—mad.

The Rich Man's Route
Many women chose to travel the Bering Sea route. After leaving Canadian and US ports, steamships ploughed north along the coast and turned east to St. Michael, Alaska. From there, travellers transferred to sternwheelers for the long trip south along the Yukon River.

While offering the least strenuous way to reach the Klondike, the water route was also the most expensive.

Stampeders who disembarked at Wrangell, Juneau or Skagway, Alaska, could only watch with envy as other, more affluent hopefuls waved them goodbye and sailed on up the coast. Nettie Hoven, the young New Yorker on the run from her lover, was a fortunate exception. As Nettie worked for her passage, the audacious working-class woman enjoyed many of the benefits of the leisure set.

The sea voyage to St. Michael was a leisurely, but tedious, three-week affair. However, when the two gold ships that sparked the rush arrived in San Francisco and Seattle in mid-July, even those who set out immediately scarcely had time to reach their destination before freeze-up. Once winter held the Yukon River highway in its grip, almost all travel ceased as sternwheelers became frozen in the ice. Passengers aboard locked-in ships would be forced to winter over for months in Circle City or other hamlets, or they could walk the rest of the way over the frozen river, against wind and snow, in temperatures as low as –70°C. In the fall of 1897, 1,800 early stampeders on board various sternwheelers awoke to find that their vessels would not move again until spring breakup.

The Ashcroft and Stikine Trails
Many Canadian stampeders wanted to avoid the customs duties applied when entering American ports on the Alaska coast. Some chose the Ashcroft Trail, which ran more than 625 kilometres north through BC, from Vancouver through the Cariboo and into the Yukon.

Only a handful of the 1,500 people who set out along the Ashcroft Trail reached their destination. Even fewer of the 3,000 starving horses, tormented by flies and mosquitoes, survived the trip. After months of exhausting travel, one hopeful finally reached the Stikine River, only to be told by Native people that he would have to travel another 600 kilometres before reaching the gold creeks. The weary traveller reached for his gun and blew out his brains.

Of the thousands who first stepped onto the old wharf in Wrangell, Alaska, only a few hundred managed to set their packs down in Dawson City. In that small number were Kate Ryan, Faith Fenton and the VON nurses. Sending dispatches off to her newspaper whenever she could, Fenton painted her readers a vivid picture of the Alaska port:

> There are no streets—each building, shack or tent, has squatted at will and everybody strolls through everybody else's backyard. The population is just as much of a pepperpot sprinkle. The lady doctor from Los Angeles, with professional bag in hand, steps blithely out of her tent quarters to visit a patient in a six-bunked, single-roomed shanty across the way. Two young lawyers are having a game of poker on a soap-box inside the doorway of their "office." Klondikers in the regulation yellow knee boots and sombrero are everywhere and the smell of pine boards and the sound of the hammer and plane is over it all.

For these women, and thousands of men, the initial destination was the Stikine Trail. Travellers who disembarked at Wrangell, Alaska, headed overland northeast to the tiny tent town of Glenora. Here, the Stikine and Ashcroft trails met. The word "trail" hardly described the slushy, mushy mess that men, women and beasts slipped and slithered over as they journeyed north beyond the Stikine River, through Glenora and Telegraph Creek to Teslin Lake and their ultimate destination, the Yukon.

Four days after leaving Vancouver, former St. Paul's Hospital nurse Kate Ryan disembarked from a coastal steamer at Wrangell. Bound for the Stikine Trail, the intrepid young woman would soon operate a series of canvas-roofed restaurants. The first leg of her journey took her up the Stikine River in the desolate northwest corner of BC. When Kate and thousands of others made the winter trip, river travel was treacherous. Deceptive ice on the frozen waterway led many to a watery grave. By the time Kate reached the small Yukon tent city of Whitehorse, the stout-hearted woman had been on the trail for more than a year.

A few months after Kate began her travels, the dauntless VON nurses, newspaper reporter Faith Fenton and thousands of other gold-hungry travellers disembarked and began hiking along the treacherous trail. In the spring of 1898, Faith, the VON contingent and the Yukon Field Force easily accomplished this leg of the trip. Travellers simply stepped aboard one of 17 paddlewheelers that plied the waters of the

Stikine River. Not long after they stepped off the boat, Faith began to hear "ominous reports" from returning travellers about the journey they had just begun. "The hum of the mosquito is over it all . . . these vampires among insects. With protecting mosquito veil and gloves worn through morning and evening hours, we live in modest comfort," Faith wrote. But there was no comfort in the low-lying swamps that lay ahead. Nurse Georgia Powell reported to Lady Aberdeen:

> From mountain to swamp and bog—bogs into whose cold, damp, mossy depths we would sink up to our knees. Swamps where we trampled down bushes and shrubs to make footing for ourselves, and where the mules stick many times, often as many as twenty all down at once, sometimes having to be unpacked . . . our baggage dumped in the mud, and where the mosquitoes held high revelry. Let me say right here, for number, size and ferocity these mosquitoes cannot be exaggerated, and despite leggings, gloves and the inevitable veil, we were badly bitten.

Faith and the nurses arose as early as 2 a.m. each day and, as Georgia reported, "went tramping, leaping, springing and climbing, a strain only the strongest and most sinewy women could bear."

Thousands had hit the trail, excited and relieved by news that Minister of the Interior Clifford Sifton had signed a tentative contract with builders to construct a 95-kilometre railroad from the head of the Stikine River to Teslin Lake. From the lakehead, a fleet of steamboats would placidly ferry prospectors into the Yukon. Unfortunately, the Senate balked at the cost. In the summer of 1898, work on the proposed railway was suddenly abandoned. Confronted with the muddy, narrow track that wound its way into the wilderness, bitter gold seekers scornfully labelled the proposed easy route "the Stikine-Teslin Joke."

The Trails from Edmonton

Thanks to the telegraph, the civilized world knew about the gold finds just days after *Excelsior* landed the first Klondike millionaires at San Francisco. Less than 300 kilometres from the port city, gold-fever victims in Fresno, California, left for the north almost immediately. G.E. Garner headed one of five Fresno groups. Twenty had signed on with Garner, and his wife Nellie wasn't about to stay at home, worrying and wondering about her husband.

Petite and demure, Nellie's appearance belied a true Klondike spirit. She was young, stronger than she looked, and she was going to get some of that gold! She would be the first of about twenty women who eventually hit the Klondike trail out of the little town of Edmonton.

The first leg of the Garners' trip north was easy. They waved goodbye to friends and family at the railway station and stepped up onto the Southern Pacific. They boarded the Canadian Pacific in Calgary, but while rolling north to Edmonton, they realized their leader and guide, J.S. Mack, had, as the *Fresno Daily Evening Expositor* put it, "skipped by the light of the moon," taking a good deal of the group's money with him. Nevertheless, barely a month after word of the Yukon gold discoveries got out, the Garner party arrived in Edmonton, ready to hit the trail. But first, there was some celebrating to do.

"It seemed as though everyone in the town was at the hotel to welcome us," Nellie wrote to family back in California, "and before leaving Edmonton . . . a large crowd of well-wishers surrounded and gave us a sort of 'Fourth of July' reception . . . A couple of photographers took my pictures in different poses and attire, and a local author is going to write a book about our party. It will be illustrated." At least two of those photographs—one of which shows a determined-looking Nellie sitting astride her horse—still exist as sad reminders of what would eventually come to pass.

The Garners' rousing send-off at Edmonton should have come as no surprise. Businessmen all over North America were eager to hitch their fortunes to the frantic quest for yellow ore. The good merchants of Edmonton's Jasper Avenue were no exception. They eagerly promoted Edmonton as the "back door" to the gold creeks. "The people of this part of the country make every inducement to those wishing to travel to Alaska," Nellie wrote to folks back home in California. "They desire them to come this way." The celebrities enjoyed their first, easy days on the trail, making an average of 20 kilometres before sunset.

"Tea parties were planned, and I received any number of invitations to attend them," Nellie wrote after another day on horseback. "All along the road and at stopping places, people stare at our party . . . and I often hear them say, 'There goes the woman who is bound for Alaska.'"

Many people, including Nellie, referred to the stampeders' destination as Alaska. For most, the Alaskan outposts of St. Michael, Skagway and Dyea were merely stops on the way to the richest land on earth, which lay hundreds of kilometres east of the international boundary between Alaska and the Yukon. All-Canadian routes such as the one the Garners chose led nowhere near Alaska. An Alaskan destination would have added weeks to their travels.

It scarcely mattered, however. Some of the routes out of Edmonton were longer than the fabled Oregon Trail. The Garners' overland route was almost 2,000 kilometres long. Even before they left Fresno, the Garners had the foresight to realize they would never reach Dawson City before both snow and temperatures fell. They would have to winter over someplace along the trail. Others were more easily misled.

"You don't need a couple of thousand dollars to start for the Klondike by the Edmonton route," calculated Joe Ladue, Dawson City's founder. A tireless Klondike booster, Joe had no hesitation in telling readers of his *Klondyke Facts*, "All you need is a good constitution, some experience in boating and camping and about $150."

A Canadian guidebook told of a road that led from Edmonton to far-off Fort Selkirk on the Yukon River. The road was fiction. A few days from town, most stampeders discovered the route they had chosen before leaving home had no discernable trail. "Hell can't be worse than this trail. I'll chance it," one suicidal traveller explained on a sign he had tacked to a tree. Travellers discovered his dead body lying beneath his final message.

Just three weeks out of Edmonton, the Garners found that their own trail had disappeared in a jungle of windfalls and a morass of muskeg. It took hours of work to free the horses from the sucking quagmires. Many animals were too exhausted to continue and were abandoned. One of the Garner party, J. Wilber Cate, decided to call it quits right then and there. "We lost so many horses that it soon became evident that we could not all get through," he told the *Expositor*, back in Fresno. "I accordingly sold my remaining horses and outfit to T. J. Kelly, my partner."

Cate didn't know it, but by the time he was telling his story to the newspaper reporter, winter had already stopped the Garner party at the remote outpost of Spirit River. Three managed to travel a little farther north and holed up at what is now Fort St. John, BC. They had travelled less than 400 kilometres, and in that distance, 94 of their 120 horses had perished.

Months later, the Garners were still pushing on. By July, more than half the distance to their Dawson City destination still lay before them, representing weeks of additional travel. However, two members of the remaining party had come down with scurvy and would have died without medical attention. Reluctantly, many of the group turned back, including the Garners. It was a life-saving decision.

With a Fort St. John doctor's care and a better diet, the two men recovered from their scurvy within days. By the time the returning stampeders reached Edmonton, more than a year had passed since they had stepped off the train. Nellie and G.E. weren't in the mood to celebrate, although they had good reason to: they were alive. Others were not so fortunate.

About 1,500 stampeders left Edmonton for the Klondike. More than 70 died either on the trail or soon after their arrival in Dawson City. Some committed suicide. Others drowned or died of injuries, but most suffered painful, lingering deaths due to scurvy. Only half of those who started out on the long trail from Edmonton finally finished the trip. Among them was that gold-fevered couple from Chicago, A.C. and Emily Craig.

On the advice of their "experienced" expedition manager, who had actually never travelled beyond the Chicago city limits, the Craigs chose the McKenzie Trail. The route turned out to be one of the longest available, meandering up rivers and across lakes over a huge expanse of territory north of the

Arctic Circle. Once this northern leg had been completed, travellers turned south and made the remaining 1,500 kilometres of the trip down the Yukon River to Dawson City.

As the only female of their group, the chore of cooking fell to Emily. After a day of backbreaking travel, the men's work ended, whereas Emily continued to toil over the campfire every night, feeding a less-than-appreciative gang of 13 men. Two months after they set out, the quarrelling group split up. Their manager, like the Garners', had abandoned the group, taking the stampeders' money with him.

The group pressed on. By the time the ordeal was over, the Craigs had survived near-starvation, muskeg and whitewater rapids. They had endured arduous portages that involved pulling their heavy boats along on log rollers and sledding across the dangerous ice of Great Slave Lake. They spent two long winters at isolated outposts and battled a fire that destroyed their tent and nearly all of Emily's clothing. By the time Emily and A.C. finally reached their destination, they were alone. Every other member of their party had given up long before. By the time the tenacious couple stepped off the steamer gangway and onto Dawson City's Front Street, the Craigs had been on the trail for two years. They arrived to find that the Klondike Gold Rush was over.

Years later, Emily betrayed no trace of bitterness when she remembered the time when she and A.C. "were alone and free . . . when nature's scenery was grand and the very solitude drew us together."

The Craigs weren't destined to remain together after their arrival in civilization. They had only been in Dawson a few weeks when news came upriver of enormous finds on the beaches of Nome, Alaska. A.C. still burned with gold fever. This time, he packed up to chase the dream alone. Emily remained in Dawson, "wishing I was back in Chicago and wondering why I came." When she earned enough money for her steamer passage, she joined A.C. in Nome, the North's newest gold-rush city.

Years after her husband died, Emily remained in Alaska, employed as a hospital worker in Anchorage. There, she met and married Dr. J.H. Romig, and the couple later retired to Colorado.

The Twin Passes

The cheapest, most direct routes to the Klondike wound through a pair of Alaska mountain passes, the Chilkoot Pass and the White Pass. At their trailheads, the passes were less than five kilometres apart. During the Klondike Gold Rush, towns were built at the waterfront starting points for each pass. Dyea became the jumping-off point for those braving the Chilkoot. Almost overnight, a town of 10,000 sprang up.

Skagway became the lawless port of call for steamers disgorging hopefuls who then slogged up the White Pass. Although longer, the White Pass had a gentler ascent than the Chilkoot. Stampeders could pack supplies on the backs of animals rather than on the backs of men. However, the route was new, and as the rain fell, the trampling by thousands of hooves, boots and shoes turned the soft forest floor into a mire of muck. Animals became trapped in mud up to their bellies.

"My heart ached for . . . the poor patient horses, burros, oxen and dogs that were bruised and bleeding until the trail was simply a trail of blood," recalled a 40-year-old divorcee who travelled up the White Pass with three other women. "The strain and hardships told on the men and many of them were cruel beyond description."

Impatient, gold-hungry men abandoned hundreds of starving, bargain-rate animals that they had bought in Seattle and Victoria. Hundreds more, their bones snapped by rocks, died screaming and snorting in agony. Others slipped and fell—or, as onlookers contended, simply walked off the trail's edge to smash themselves in the rocky gullies of Dead Horse Gulch.

Prostitute "Dutch" Kate Wilson had been the first white woman to trudge up the Chilkoot Trail, with a group of prospectors in 1888. A few years later, Anna DeGraf, Ethel Berry and Belinda Mulrooney braved the pass. Now, at the height of the rush, Martha Purdy, Nellie Cashman, Ethel Berry (for the second time, accompanied by her teenaged sister, Edna "Tot" Bush) and a few hundred other women were conquering what came to be called "the Trail of '98," a trail that proved to be an impossible ordeal for many men. These women simply persevered against all odds, determined to reach a better, or at least different, life in the Klondike.

Belinda Mulrooney and her group pause on the trail.

The Chilkoot offered the kind of severe test of physical stamina that few stampeders had ever endured, and no one who faced the Chilkoot would ever forget it. "I was straining every nerve, every ounce of physical endurance in that ever upward climb," Martha Purdy remembered. "There were moments when, with sweating forehead, pounding heart and panting breath, I felt I could go no further."

60

Martha's brother George accompanied her on the trail. George attempted to comfort and encourage his sister. Finally, his patience broke, and the exhausted man screamed, "For God's sake, Polly, buck up and be a man! Have some style and move on!" Incensed, Martha "bucked up" and reached the summit.

Martha Purdy and other stampeders choosing the Chilkoot found what the former Chicago socialite called a "good wagon road," criss-crossing the milky green Taiya River through the coastal rain forest. About 18 kilometres up the trail, conditions changed dramatically. From then on, Martha recalled, "we realized we were indeed on a trail of heartbreaks and dead hopes."

When she first heard about gold strikes in the Klondike, Belinda Mulrooney was just 24 years old, but already a seasoned businesswoman thanks to her profitable restaurant venture. Once again, thanks to her love of business, Belinda was in the right place at the right time.

The former steamship stewardess was operating a Seattle retailer's outlet at Juneau, Alaska, when she heard rumours about the Klondike strikes. Was there any truth to them? A visitor from the Yukon was wintering over in Juneau, and Belinda sought him out. Dave "Two Fingers" McKay proved to be an ideal contact: he was an eyewitness to something the rest of the world would not know about until the following summer. As she told others years later, Belinda made a habit of being "nice to anyone with knowledge."

In late summer of 1896, McKay had been one of the small number of Yukon prospectors to hear about George Carmack's initial discovery on what had been called Rabbit Creek. McKay had been among the initial group of Rabbit prospectors to rename the creek "Bonanza," and, with nothing more than a humble piece of rope, he had assisted the others in measuring out their claims. McKay had spent the summer washing out his gold, which he was now spending in Juneau.

A credible witness such as McKay made what others called rumours into something Belinda Mulrooney was prepared to call fact. She knew any future gold rush represented a huge business opportunity. But, she reasoned, rich prospectors who had a lot of money to spend would likely prefer to spend it as close to their diggings as possible. Belinda Mulrooney needed to be where her future customers were: in the Klondike.

The young entrepreneur quickly organized a group to head up the Chilkoot Pass. However, after reaching the trail Belinda realized she had neither the men nor the resources needed for the trip. She abandoned the project.

On April Fool's Day, 1897, four months before gold fever swept North America, Belinda returned to the pass, better equipped to meet the Chilkoot's main challenge—the formidable 45-degree climb from Sheep Camp to the mountaintop. Just 2.5 kilometres from camp, the summit soared 1,100 metres into the sky, rising 300 metres in less than one kilometre.

It was impossible to carry the necessary food and supplies in merely one trip. Stampeders had to climb the pass over and over again, often making more than 30 trips and taking up to eight weeks of backbreaking effort to bring what was needed over the summit. "Relaying was endless," Belinda recalled. "They'd make one trip up to the top and knew they'd have to relay to get sufficient food for one year. Before they'd make the round trip they'd give up and say, 'impossible.'"

Always ready to seize an opportunity, Belinda took advantage of the daunting climb that defeated so many others. "After our camp was placed, I got to buying supplies from the disheartened people who looked at the summit . . . such a small percentage made the summit," she explained. "A great many returned, some snowblind, some . . . sick or homesick." Belinda paid the desperate and dejected only a fraction of what their supplies had originally cost them. Later, the opportunistic entrepreneur would charge much more in her Dawson City store for some of the same merchandise.

Months later, on the same trail, California widow Georgia White, who had left her children behind, took comfort from a bottle as she climbed. By the time she and a friend reached the summit, the bottle was empty but the light-headed ladies had conquered the pass. The last leg had taken them an exhausting 11 hours.

At Sheep Camp, Mae McKamish Meadows and her sharpshooter husband, Charley, pitched their tent and waited for their outfit to be packed over the summit. Within hours, Mother Nature turned nasty. At 6:30 a.m., a landslide halfway up the summit let loose a torrent of mud and water on the unsuspecting camp below, carrying away tents, provisions and supplies—including the Meadows' liquor and casino outfits—as well as the lives of three gold seekers. "People saw the flood coming—could see a black dust and trees falling everywhere. No one thought it would be so bad," Mae confessed. "Charley went out, took a look . . . He came running in and said the flood was there and to run for my life."

Mae scrambled for her clothes and grabbed a small suitcase. The two narrowly escaped. "We were about three yards away when the tent went down," she explained. "Well, I wanted to stop and see the water, and to try to button my clothes, but Charley kept saying to go on farther up, so I had to keep on running. If we had not got out at that moment we would have been drowned. It was terrible. Charley said if he had a Kodac [a photograph] of me as I was running from Sheeps Camp flood, there would not be any use of going to the Klondike, as that would have been a gold mine in itself."

Not even Mae Meadows could make light of what happened near the same place the following spring. In February and March 1898, storms dumped many feet of wet snow over the Chilkoot Pass. On April 2 and 3, many Chilkat packers retreated to the lower reaches of the trail, below Sheep Camp. Soon afterward, less than two kilometres above the camp, hundreds of thousands of tons of snow broke loose and cascaded down the pass, obliterating the long lines of men and women struggling up the slope.

"Everybody rushed to the slide to help dig out those who were buried and were able to save some of them," Ethel Berry's sister, Tot, remembered. "A man and his wife were buried in the slide; she was taken out alive and directed them to where her husband was buried. They had just brought him to the surface when somebody yelled that another slide was coming and the workers all had to run for their lives. The rescued man was buried again and he wasn't found after the second slide." Only a handful of victims were uncovered alive. Even while others attempted to rescue those who were trapped, the long line of stampeders reformed and continued its painful shuffle up the slope.

In Sheep Camp, a long, white canvas tent was erected. A hastily scribbled sign near the front flap identified it as the morgue. Inside were the frozen remains of dozens of victims. Estimates vary, but at least 70 people lost their lives in the Palm Sunday avalanche, enough to fill a new cemetery near Dyea. Many bodies were not revealed until weeks later, when spring temperatures rose and the snow receded.

Those who staggered to the top of the Chilkoot or White pass had little energy or inclination to reflect on their victory. Exhausted and aching, they might have felt beaten and defeated. Any celebration was tempered by the knowledge that they were still hundreds of kilometres from their Klondike objective.

5

The Other Side
of the Mountains

WEARY TREKKERS TRUDGED ACROSS THE broad, treeless, rock and pond landscape of the summit. They were all numbed by the thought that regardless of how exhausted they were, the journey had barely begun. Thousands of miles from their homes, every man and woman who had scaled the mountain faced a hard, bitter truth. Many days of travel—and who knew how many dangers—lay ahead before they would set foot in Dawson City.

The Way Down
"Then the descent! Down ever downward," Martha Purdy recalled. The vast land on the other side of the summit was dotted with a series of large bodies of water, beginning

with Crater Lake at the very base of the mountain and Lake Lindeman a few kilometres north. "The last two miles into Lindeman was the most excruciating struggle of the whole trip," Martha Purdy later wrote. "Rocks! Rocks! Rocks! Tearing boots to pieces. Hands bleeding from scratches. I can bear it no longer. In my agony I beg the men to leave me." Martha's brother, George, carried her in his arms for the final leg of the journey.

Martha and George made their trek in the summer. Travelling down the mountain was considerably faster—and certainly more exhilarating—in winter. The earliest stampeders merely slid their horses down the eastern slope of the Chilkoot. Men and women also slid down the slope, while those with heavily packed sleds exerted all their energy to keep their loads from running loose down the mountain. Tot Bush tobogganed down on a board, laughing with delight. Such momentary frivolity was merely a brief respite in an otherwise daunting journey.

The Tent Town of Lake Bennett

Crater Lake was small; Martha Purdy and many Chilkoot stampeders walked around it on their way to the Klondike. However, boating was another option. Boat building began in earnest on the shores of the first navigable lake in the Yukon, the scenic 16-kilometre-long Lake Bennett. The voyage down the King River from Lake Lindeman into Lake Bennett was short but furious, as the white water of One-Mile Rapids churned along the river's twisting course.

Those who arrived at Lake Lindeman in the autumn of 1897 and 1898 had no time to enjoy the scenery. They were obsessed with the need to build a boat or flat-bottomed scow quickly. It was a race against the calendar. Stampeders who knew nothing of carpentry or construction built flimsy crafts. Soon, the river was littered with the remains of rafts, boats and precious, waterlogged possessions.

"There is not much time to rest or anything," Wild West performer Mae Meadows related to her sister in far-off Santa Cruz, California. "Do not know how long it will take to build two boats. May get a chance to write again . . . It is getting pretty late and it will take a lot of hurrying to get over the lake before it freezes." In closing, Mae added, "Well, I must get out and see the town. I can hear hammers everywhere, it is the busiest little town I ever saw. People are hurrying off [to the Klondike] every day."

The "town" of Mae's letter was nothing more than a huge semicircle of white tents, stretching along the curving shorelines and dotting the lower reaches of the slopes. Soon, tents covered both banks of the little river between Lindeman and Bennett. By May, the tent city of 5,000 boasted at least one legitimate street lined with canvas hotels, saloons and doctors' and lawyers' offices.

Those who arrived later, walking through the small spruce grove high above the river, could hear the town before they saw it, the ringing of hammers and the rasp of saws floating up the slopes. As newcomers approached the crest of the hill, near a half-completed church, trees were being felled all around them. Soon the lakeside banks were completely denuded. Sweating men carried or rolled freshly cut logs to curious-looking rough frameworks called Armstrong sawmills.

One man stood perched on elevated scaffolding, holding the upper end of a long whipsaw, while his partner on the ground below gripped the other end. Up and down they heaved the saw, cutting through a newly chopped log only on the down stroke, the man above desperately trying to keep his balance while attempting to keep the saw blade along a straight line. The man below, standing in a blizzard of sawdust, tried to keep his temper in check. Dozens of partnerships ended acrimoniously in Bennett's Armstrong sawmills.

Some parties paid other travellers to build their boats. Resourceful Belinda Mulrooney had come prepared, carrying the fibrous, oiled hemp used to make boats waterproof. "I had materials for boat building, and that stuff they pack boats with, oakum. All I had to do was to exchange that for labour. Pretty soon we had big boats all dolled up and named."

By 1898, commercial sawmills had been established. Martha Purdy and her party were customers. "In three weeks our boat was finished," she wrote. "She was a fine unpainted craft shaped like a fisherman's dory and built of Alaska pine at King's Shipyard, Lake Bennett, at a cost of

$275. She was 11-and-a-half metres across the bottom, and two-and-a-half metres at the top. In a short time our goods were loaded. When our several tons of luggage and our party of six got in, there was very little space above the water-line and very little room inside. However, we sailed away in drenching rain."

Downriver to Dawson City

Some 14 months before Martha's party launched its boat at Bennett, Belinda Mulrooney stared out at the still-frozen surface of the lake and knew she was in a race against time. Once news of the strikes reached the outside, a tide of humanity was sure to wash up on Skagway and Dyea beaches. Belinda had to reach the Klondike quickly in order to be ready for business when the hordes arrived. Yet it would be weeks before rising temperatures thawed the ice.

"We didn't wait for Bennett to be opened," Belinda explained years later. "We put the boats on the sleds and pushed on . . . That lake stuff was easy going. There was quite a number of hours of sun and if the sleighs got stuck, we put a dog on to pull. When the wind filled the sails again the group simply unharnessed the dog, and threw him on the boat."

The following autumn, as Mae Meadows and her group were building their boat at Bennett, summer sunshowers turned to snow. Every passing day increased the risk that boaters would be trapped in a frozen river halfway to Dawson City. Men worked at a frenzied pace. Mae, Charley and their companions finally pushed off the gravel beach on October 18, while others stood by and shook their heads in disbelief. It was a close call: the group got to within 50 kilometres of Dawson then awoke one morning to find the Yukon River frozen solid. Undaunted, they took the boats apart, built sleds and pulled much of their gear down the frozen river and into the gold town.

Sledding down the ice should have been a fairly simple task, but the Yukon River was not the smooth skating rink most trekkers imagined. Huge hummocks of ice formed as the surface thawed and refroze throughout the fall. Great ice pinnacles, often four metres high, dotted the eerie, white landscape.

Mae and Charley Meadows had skidded easily over the ice between Lake Marsh and Lake Laberge. By June, the ice had vanished, and the river seethed and foamed through two sets of major whitewater: Miles Canyon and White Horse Rapids.

In the spring of 1898, on their return trip to the Klondike, Ethel and Clarence "C.J." Berry left a little too late to sled down the lakes. By the time the Berry party started out across Lake Laberge, the last link in the Yukon lake chain, the weather had warmed alarmingly. Less courageous souls would have put ashore, but the Berrys mushed on. Ethel's sister, Tot Bush, wrote later:

We hugged the shore more closely each day. As there

was constant danger of the ice breaking, we carried long poles; in the case we should find thin ice the poles would prevent us from going through.

When C.J. halted the sled to wait for us, he noticed that the runner was in water. Oh, boy! They used the whip on the dogs and worked like mad to keep the sleds moving. When Ethel felt the ice waving, she stopped, which was the worst thing she could do. Clarence looked back to see if we had noticed what was wrong with the sleds . . . He couldn't leave the dogs and the sleds to come to her aid and so he yelled, "For God's sake Ethel, RUN!"

Tot grabbed her sister by the hand, and the two women dashed for shore. With each step, the heaving ice made it like "being on the ocean." Clarence had done the right thing in keeping the sleds moving. A dead weight would have gently opened the ice, swallowing everything and possibly everyone. The next day, the group received a sober reminder of their narrow escape; a man and his dogs had gone through the ice not far away.

The ice began to move out of Lake Bennett on May 29, 1898. North-West Mounted Police commander Sam Steele walked up the hill behind his office to see "the wonderful exodus of the boats." He counted more than 800 on the water that morning. Old-timers who had made the trip through the lakes and down the Yukon River doubted that many of the thousands of men who set off that morning and in the days that followed would make it to their destination. What chance did a woman have?

Not long after the breakup on Bennett, Commander Steele took a steamer trip through the lakes and down the Yukon River. At the little settlement of Canyon City, just a few minutes ride above the entrance to Miles Canyon, he learned from the local police detachment that more than 150 boats had been smashed in the river's rapids, and 10 men had drowned. The police themselves had rescued a number of women and children too.

Steele made a snap decision and decreed that no women or children would be allowed in boats on the canyon's three treacherous kilometres of rapids. "If they are strong enough to come to the Klondike," he told an assembled crowd, "they can walk the five miles of grassy bank to the foot of the White Horse." For $25.05 per pound of cargo, a horse-drawn tram would portage a boat around the rapids.

Like all other stampeders, Martha Purdy and her group stopped at the NWMP post on the short river between Lake Tagish and Lake Marsh. She was astonished to learn from a young policeman that during the previous 12 months alone, 18,000 people had stopped for customs inspections. According to the police tally, Martha was the 631st woman to make her way to the Klondike.

Martha's group successfully navigated Miles Canyon before they were swept into the White Horse Rapids. For some, the ride was exhilarating. One woman did it twice,

Dwarfed by towering walls of basalt rock, travellers such as Frances Dorley and Martha Purdy braved the churning water of Miles Canyon, on the Yukon River.

just for fun, saying afterwards, "I do not know when I ever enjoyed anything so much in my life."

For others like Martha, it was a heart-stopping experience. "Half-way through, our steering oar broke with a crack like that of a pistol shot, above the roaring waters. For a tense moment, the boat whirled half her length about in the current. Captain Spencer quickly seized another oar, calling coolly, 'Never mind, boys! Let her go stern to.' A second's hesitation and our lives would have paid the penalty."

Frances Dorley, who had escaped her mundane Seattle life and her cloying parents, had travelled nearly without incident until she approached Lake Tagish. There, she discovered that her "neat, expensive boat, made of soft cedar, was slowly coming apart at the seams." It was a common problem. Once ashore, the men she travelled with set to work to reinforce the boat, while plucky Frances "baked a batch of bread over a campfire and caught some fish." However, farther up the river, not far from the northern end of Lake Laberge, four rocky outcroppings rose high above the river's swiftly flowing waters. The resulting channels had been christened "Five Fingers Rapids." Here, Frances Dorley learned how little her prudent opinion mattered to her male companions. She had read a book in Skagway about the dangers of the river and how best to navigate through the Five Fingers. She suggested the group choose the channel farthest west.

"The little Scot, McChord, hooted at what he called my 'book-learned knowledge' and shouted that I, being a woman, could know nothing about navigation. With true masculine loyalty, the other men sided with him."

As the boat tossed this way and that in the churning waters, discretion proved to be the better part of male valour, and two of the men quickly decided they had better row across to the safer channel. "We all grabbed oars and began rowing frantically with all our strength," Frances reported. "We managed to force our way through the turbulent white foam until we were in midstream."

They were too late. Further exertion against the current was pointless. Mere seconds from the worst of the rapids, and with one huge island outcropping looming closer, another in the party suggested to the terrified group that they try to shoot through the centre channel. "I closed my eyes, said a little prayer and tried to hold fast to my ebbing courage," Frances recalled. "Then we were shooting with brutal speed through the giant finger."

Miraculously, the flimsy boat and its passengers emerged from Five Fingers intact, and a few kilometres later they easily manoeuvred through Rink Rapids. By this time, Frances and her companions had reached the halfway point in their Yukon River voyage. Once through the White Horse Rapids, the remaining river voyage to Dawson City would prove to be smooth sailing.

Despite harsh conditions, horrific trails and rushing rapids, the women who had reached Dawson City were ready to make their fortunes.

6

Leaving It All Behind

WHEN WOMEN TRAVELLED TO THE Klondike, they often had little hint of the severe changes their lives were about to undergo. Quite apart from the brutal physical hardship of the trail, they also endured unexpected psychological stress. Tolerances were stretched to the breaking point and dispositions soured. Wilderness living conditions called into question almost everything the women had taken for granted during their former lives on the outside.

Klondike Fashions

One of the first visible signs of women's discomfiture was the sudden conflict over how they were expected—or how they wanted—to dress once they disembarked from their trains or steamships.

Decorous and voluminous, women's fashions were totally unfit for life on the trail. Vintage photos of Faith Fenton and the VON nurses show them sporting the narrow-brimmed hats popular during the era. The women might have been in vogue on New York's Fifth Avenue, but in a place where practicality could mean the difference between life and death, or at least between comfort and misery, these tiny hats were a symbol of the silliness of fashion.

Wide skirts that carefully hid everything but the soles of one's shoes were not designed for traversing deadfalls. Whalebone corsets that ensured a woman's "wasp waist" rendered their wearers breathless and faint after even the most modest exertion across streams and over boulders.

Ethel Berry and others made serious attempts to pack practical clothes. In her bride's trousseau, she packed articles made of "good, strong, warm, substantial material that could stand the wear and tear of a year, and maybe more, in that bitter cold country." Ethel's choices were undoubtedly influenced by her new husband, Clarence, who had lived in the Yukon for years. Few had the advantage of insight.

In Juneau, Belinda Mulrooney conversed with men who knew the Klondike. As a result, she had some of her wardrobe, including an eider and fox-fur sleeping bag, custom made in Seattle. Along with "short" calf-length skirts and men's-style shirts, Belinda also packed snow glasses to diminish the glare that left many stampeders blind. "I ditched the corsets," she recalled, "which was a rash thing to do in those days. I suffered a lot from the whalebone stuff. I always had a grudge against it."

While still in Chicago preparing for her trek, Martha Purdy tried to make practical wardrobe choices, one of which was "a skirt of shockingly immodest length (it actually showed my ankles)." Yet Purdy's upper-class status dictated that she also include, as she put it, "a blouse with a high stiff collar almost to my ears, and a pair of voluminous brown silk bloomers, which came below the knee." In an age where the sight of an ankle was provocative, all prudent women wore bloomers or knickers under their skirts to guard against the accidental exposure of shapely white flesh. Once on the trail, these women railed against social convention and the customary confining, concealing clothing.

Within a day or two of her arrival in the Yukon, Martha gave up many of her fashionable clothes. "I shed my sealskin jacket," Martha confessed. "I cursed my hot, high, buckram collar, my tight heavily boned corsets, my long corduroy skirt, my full bloomers which I had to hitch up with every step."

Gold-camp veteran Nellie Cashman did the unheard of: she wore pants. Nellie didn't care what anybody else thought and knew better than most what worked and what didn't. She had "roughed it" many times in the past, in Colorado, Arizona and Nevada. Over 20 years earlier, she had endured the winter trail into BC's Cassiar gold camps, heading a rescue mission to save scurvy-suffering prospectors.

"You would like to know how I dress when on such expeditions, eh?" Nellie slyly taunted a *Daily Colonist* reporter in Victoria, as she prepared for her conquest of the Klondike. She knew the reporter wanted to hear something provocative, something that made good copy. As he scribbled, she stated nonchalantly that she dressed "in many respects as a man does, with long heavy trousers and rubber boots."

Sensitive to the fact that many would find such dress outrageous, Nellie was quick to add, "Of course, when associating with strangers, I wear a long, rubber coat." When with men who didn't care whether she wore pants or not, it's likely the coat quickly came off. And skirts?

"Skirts are out of the question up north, as many women will find out before they reach the gold fields," she warned.

By the time winter turned to summer on the Teslin Trail, Kate Ryan had exchanged her dogs for horses. Kate created a tough, culotte-style riding skirt so she could swing her leg over her mount and ride comfortably, like a man. She shortened her long mackinaw coat so that it, too, fit well while she rode on horseback. A practical, broad-brimmed straw hat, which she called her "cow breaker," shaded her face from the summer sun as she led her string of pack horses up the trail.

Predictably, many men were less than enthusiastic about these deviations in dress. In Wrangell, *Globe* reporter Faith Fenton was scolded by an American army officer who objected to her practical, knee-length skirt. Properly chastened, Faith sought out a seamstress who lengthened the skirt to her ankles. Ironically, as black satinette was the only material available for the job, the result had a more risqué effect than the original skirt.

Back in 1887, while Nellie Cashman was getting ready to head to Australia in search of diamonds, a woman named "Dutch" Kate Wilson was on her way north. Dutch Kate, a prostitute, was accompanying a group of prospectors through the Chilkoot Pass to the Yukon River gold town of Fortymile, 84 kilometres downstream from the future site of Dawson City. As the only woman in that tiny hamlet, Kate enjoyed a monopoly of her particular trade, an advantage not enjoyed by other "ladies of easy virtue" who later stumbled up the passes during the rush. Her travelling companions likely never forgot her, nor the particular "shame" they thought she endured on the trail. "The poor creature, in order to better enable her to undergo the hardships of the trip, had donned male attire," one of the party, John Rogers, piously reported to *The Daily Alaskan*.

Poor creature? Only in the minds of men such as Rogers, who unintentionally revealed Kate's pragmatic, practical clothes sense. As the group floated downriver toward a Native village, Rogers recalled, Kate hastily doffed her masculine duds and "arrayed herself in her finest apparel, powdered her face and arranged her bangs in her most bewitching style." Kate's exotic appearance had a stunning effect on the Natives. "They greeted her with exclamations of delight," Rogers said.

Rogers obviously couldn't believe that a woman would endure the privations of the trail out of anything but desperation and referred to her again as, "This unfortunate woman," who, he then admits, "had a series of adventures during that summer that would read like a romance." Scandalous!

By 1899, weary Edmonton Trail veterans Emily Craig and her husband had finally arrived on the Yukon River. They booked passage on a paddlewheeler bound for Dawson City, where civilization's trappings had arrived some time before. After their disastrous tent fire, Emily's husband had purchased a beaded buckskin dress, fur cap and moccasins to replace Emily's clothing. Warm and wear resistant, it was the perfect outfit for the rugged wilderness. As they waited for the steamer, Emily saw other women on their way to "the city."

"It was a sight to see the dresses and hats that the ladies, going through here, were wearing," Emily later remembered. "There was no white woman's clothing in these parts, and it seemed everyone was looking at me. I wanted to cry, but that would not make it any better . . . and I wanted some new dresses before I got to Dawson."

Less than a month earlier, the ceremonial last spike of the White Pass and Yukon Railway had been driven into the rail tie at Lake Bennett. Now, women bound for the Klondike could simply lift their long, fashionable dresses and step daintily up the black iron steps of a Skagway train coach. They would sit in comfort, looking down at the deserted pass that so many exhausted stampeders had tramped through just months before.

Rustic Hospitality

In the late summer of 1897, John Feero, who had escaped financially depressed Washington State, was finally reunited with his wife, Emma, and their five children in Skagway. John had decided to return to the transportation business. The market was strong; men were desperate for pack animals. John was thriving in the tent-town's rough-and-ready atmosphere. When finally reunited, the family went to a big, barnlike, two-storey building for a celebration dinner. The "hotel" featured a makeshift dining room with long tables and benches. The cloakroom was nothing more than a long bench with nails in the wall.

After dinner, Emma wondered where they were to sleep. John pointed to a ladder leading to the floor above. "Huh! I can't walk up that ladder!" Emma protested primly, but to no avail. It was either go up the ladder or spend a sleepless night below. When she finished her climb, she found that nothing but canvas curtains divided the loft into rooms. Three mattresses were scattered on the rough floorboards. Surrounded by drunks on both sides of the canvas curtains, it was a sleepless night for Emma in her second-storey "bedroom."

Before breakfast, Emma looked down the ladder at the

unshaven mob slurping and munching below and told John, "I can't go down there." She quickly discovered that she must join the mob or go hungry, so down she went.

Farther up the trails, hospitality was just as crude, and hotel accommodations were even more rustic than those in Skagway. During her group's descent from the summit, Martha Purdy took supper at a cabin. She had come a long way, indeed, from dinners with china and crystal served by the hired girl in the comfortable Chicago home she had shared with her former husband, Will. Two dollars bought bean soup, ham and eggs, prunes, bread and butter and an apology from the proprietor. "The middle of it ain't done," he admitted, gesturing to the bread, "but you don't have to eat it. I hurried too much."

Martha's brother George carried her into the Tacoma Hotel at Crater Lake, and she stumbled off to a "canvas stretched on four logs, with a straw shakedown." Yet Martha was so exhausted that she later confessed, "The downiest couch in the world or the softest bed in a king's palace could not have made a better resting place for me."

Others toiling up the "trail of blood" known as the White Pass would have been envious of Martha's modest comfort. After an arduous nine-mile hike, one woman asked a fellow stampeder how far she had to travel to reach the White Pass Hotel.

"Why, bless your blue eyes," the man laughed. "There it is, a hundred feet ahead!"

"Oh, is that it?" asked the incredulous trekker. "I thought it was a horse stable or pig sty!"

Once inside, the woman asked the manager to show her to her room, as she was very tired. Her request was greeted by guffaws from the men sitting around the tables.

"Well, Miss, I've only got these two rooms," the landlord explained patiently. "One is the kitchen, the other is a barroom, dining room and settin' room. You'll have to sleep here if you stay."

She and her companion were soon joined by three other exhausted women. The owner spread blankets on the rough plank floor, and they all slept side by side—"five women with our heads under the bar."

Had the White Pass Hotel's owner heard about this exchange, he undoubtedly would have been amused. He was none other than John Feero, whose wife, Emma, had been so disgusted by her own hotel experience in Skagway just a few months earlier.

Hearth and Home

Most husbands and fathers missed their wives and families; however, many stampeders or frontier businessmen concluded that it was far better if "the missus" and little ones remained thousands of miles away from the crude northern existence. Although he left no records of his feelings, it is obvious life was never the same for John Feero after Emma and the children arrived at Skagway. John led his family to the woods behind the beachfront area that would soon be divided into boardwalk-fronted streets. The "residential area" was a collection of canvas tents scattered haphazardly among the trees. John's tent was staked out just a few feet from the horses he packed.

Emma had managed to bring three mattresses and box springs up the coast. Inside the large tent, two mattresses were placed on boxes, and the other went on posts hammered into the dirt floor. Now, the family had an under-the-bed storage space. Also, Emma had brought a stove, which was placed in a corner of the tent. There was no table, so John decided he would have to purchase lumber to make one. Even though the sawmill worked non-stop, there was not a board to be bought. Instead, John and others drove four posts into the floor, over which he nestled a rented wooden box. John went into the woods to saw the ends off some logs. Now, the family had chairs. Before long, the family's cabin had been hacked out of the trees, and they began to enjoy the rustic comforts of home.

Breaking Through the Social Barriers

Gold fever cut across every social class and ethnic background and touched people from almost every corner of the globe. Those of high social and financial positions (including the Seattle mayor, who abandoned his office without notice) headed for the Klondike with the same zeal as retail clerks and near-penniless labourers. Whether they sailed up the coast or tramped up overland trails, men and women were forced to ignore the social, cultural and language barriers that usually kept various classes and races from interacting along anything but acceptable pathways.

For decades before the Klondike Gold Rush, hardy fur traders and a few prospectors had formed friendships, trading alliances and live-in relationships with the Natives in their vicinities. When a pregnant Native woman in Circle City, Alaska, pointed a finger at one of the white prospectors, a "miners' meeting" was quickly convened, and those present gave the accused man a choice: pay the mother $500 to bring up his forthcoming child or marry the woman. He chose matrimony and soon was the father of a number of additional children. Years before the Klondike Gold Rush, there were enough "mixed blood" offspring around Fortymile that Bishop William Bompas of the Anglican Church Missionary Society began a school for the children.

However, even in this remote corner of the world, the attitudes of both Native and white people were sometimes less flexible than their casual commercial and physical mingling would suggest. When the Reverend Richard Bowen visited the Native community of Nuklako, on the future site of Dawson City, a local Han trapper told him bluntly, "Indian boy, Indian want him. White boy, white man want him. Half-breed, no Indian. No white man. Indian no want him. White man no want him."

Bishop Bompas, for one, felt that there was altogether

too much racial mingling. The mission segregated whites and Natives. The log chapel, school and the Han people themselves were located on a small island across the Yukon River from Fortymile. There is no doubt that Bompas encouraged segregation for the Natives' own protection from the prospectors and the liquor they were often eager to sell or share.

Until 1897, most Natives had yet to lay eyes on a white woman. The gold rush changed all that. While at Lake Laberge, Frances Dorley's party came upon a group of Native people selling trout to gold seekers. As members of the group clustered around to examine her, she immediately grew concerned. "Finally," Frances reported, "the chief spokesman of the group stepped forward and addressed my companions: 'Nice squaw. We like her. Which one of you does she belong to? We give you many fish and even much money, if you will leave her here with us.'"

One of the men came to Frances' rescue. "Stepping between the Indians and me he murmured nervously that I was his squaw and not for sale," Frances later recounted. "I, the 'fine squaw,' stood rooted to the spot, feeling more afraid than at any other time since leaving Seattle."

The gold rushes at Fortymile and later on the Klondike creeks brought white and Native peoples together as never before. Lonely, isolated men continued to seek Native women as personal partners. By 1895, future gold-rush millionaire Clarence Berry reported that every Fortymile prospector

Kate Carmack, in a California studio portrait, wears a gold-nugget necklace, a symbol of the Carmacks' new-found wealth.

had a Native "kootchman," or wife. The reason was obvious: there were few white women available. However, there were other practical reasons to consider a Native woman as live-in partner.

"White women are not much good, savin' your presence," a Teslin trail-packer told Faith Fenton. "They won't work. A klootchman . . . is best. She don't ask no questions and she does what she's ordered." Even in an era of male dominance, this news was likely enough to cause thousands of married male readers to pause and consider, however briefly, a future for themselves in the Klondike. But the opinionated packer had more to say.

"Can you cook?" he asked Fenton. "Can you wash blankets? And I suppose you couldn't round up cayuses? No? Well, you see, you wouldn't be no use to a packer. A Kootchman'ud be far better."

The fates of some Native women were inextricably bound to the gold rush, but only a very few profited by it in any lasting way. One of those who did was the Russian/Native wife of the man who virtually owned Circle City, Alaska. When pioneer Alaska Commercial Company trader Jack McQuesten had married Satejdenalno years before, he was 42. She was 14. The woman Jack called Katherine or Kate became the mother of the big trader's 11 children, most born in a tent outside their home ("Indian babies must always be born in the fresh air," she told Anna DeGraf). Kate was destined to be Jack's lifelong companion.

Kate McQuesten's life changed forever when news of George Carmack's Klondike strike reached Circle City during the winter of 1897. Overnight, the place became a ghost town. McQuesten and his family followed everyone else up the frozen Yukon River to the tent town that surveyor William Ogilvie called Dawson City. Too late to stake his own claim, McQuesten bought a share in an existing one, which eventually paid him $10,000 in gold, an amount it took most wage earners over a decade to make. However, it was his large A.C. Company operation in Dawson that made McQuesten truly wealthy.

By the time the Klondike Gold Rush was over, Jack and Kate had moved to a palatial home in Berkeley, California, and their children had been educated in American schools. Jack McQuesten died in 1910, but Kate's business savvy allowed her to live in comfort for the rest of her days.

Years before he made the strike that would start the gold rush, George Carmack had married a Tagish woman. His wife died soon after their traditional marriage ceremony. George's mother-in-law then arranged a marriage between George and his first wife's younger sister, Shaaw Tlaa, whom he called Kate. For years, they were happy. Together, they packed outfits from John Healy's trading post up the Chilkoot. Later, Kate managed the trading post George built near Five Fingers Rapids, the site of present-day Carmacks.

When George became rich, Kate, as his partner and mother of their daughter, Graphie, became rich too. Kate's riches—and her happiness—ended in 1898, when she accompanied George, her cousin, Tagish Charlie, and her brother, Skookum Jim, to the outside for the first time.

While in Seattle, Jim, Charlie and Kate became victims of culture shock. Kate chopped notches in the Seattle Hotel's stairway banister, "marking her trail" so she could later find her room, and indulged in what the *Seattle Post-Intelligencer* called "an aboriginal Yukon war dance" in an upstairs corridor. "Having nothing but money," the Native millionaires caused a near riot by throwing coins out the window of their hotel suite. "The streets became a seething mass of struggling humanity," the newspaper reported. "Men dived from the walks and from passing streetcars, butcher boys and teamsters hurled themselves from their seats, conductors and gripmen forgot all about their charges, policemen forgot to say 'move on.'"

The Tagish trio was jailed on drunk-and-disorderly charges. "Jim and Charlie are here and a nice time they have been making of it," George angrily wrote his sister in California. "All hands got drunk and some of them got in the cooler. I am disgusted with the whole outfit."

As a man attempting to establish himself in California business circles, George worried that his reputation would suffer. He felt he couldn't afford to be associated with his personal and professional partners any longer. Before long, he had separated from Kate and had bought out Charlie and Jim. Kate unsuccessfully attempted to sue for alimony and child support and later moved back to what is now Carcross to live near friends and family. Making Native handcrafts for visitors and living on the edge of poverty, Kate was the most visible victim of the clash of cultures brought about by the gold rush.

The tacit acceptance of cohabitation between white men and Native women changed as more white women arrived in the Klondike. Suddenly, it was unseemly for a prospector or trader to be seen living with a Native woman, and those who actually chose to live in the villages of their wives' people were scornfully called "squaw men." While his circumstances were certainly unique, George Carmack's decision to leave Kate was not uncommon. As social pressures increased, scores of early prospectors and traders, including Arthur Harper, who had been Jack McQuesten's early partner, and Joe Ladue, who joined them later, abandoned their Native wives. Given their treatment by their white "husbands," some other Native women might have wished for a similar fate.

Anna DeGraf was sleeping in her Circle City cabin when she was awakened by a "terrible rumpus" from the cabin next door. Furniture was being thrown about. A woman screamed. Anna jumped out of bed, threw something around herself and ran over.

"The door was not barred, so I opened it and entered. The man had a chair lifted above his head and was about to bring it down on the woman when I yelled at him, 'You put that chair down, and do it quick!'"

"Don't you interfere here," the enraged man warned Anna. "What business is this of yours?"

"I will interfere," Anna argued. "You stop abusing that woman or I'll go over to the [Alaska Commercial] Company and report you."

Fearful of Jack McQuesten's response (after all, Jack had married a Native woman himself), the man lowered the chair. The woman later told Anna that she and her five children had eaten nothing for two days. When she asked her husband for money, he would fly into a rage and beat her. He had spent all his money at a dance hall.

Most white women didn't want to associate with Native peoples at all, as a number of Circle City reminiscences attest. At one fundraising dance, white women refused to dance while Native women were on the floor. Another time, when the common-law white wife of a Circle City dance-hall proprietor refused to interact with the Native women in the establishment, the owner realized he had to take action or risk losing trade from the Native people. In full view of his customers, the dance-hall operator walked over and knocked his disdainful wife to the floor. As late as 1905, when the wife of the Anglican bishop gave a visiting Mayo woman a place of honour at a church tea, auxiliary members were scandalized.

Before John Feero began building his cabin, his wife, Emma, noticed that someone was building on the next lot. Emma was delighted to have neighbours nearby for company. The happy anticipation was short-lived. The next morning Emma was outraged to see a large saloon sign on the roof of the neighbours' cabin. Emma forced John to buy the building to avoid living next to a saloon and the class of men she thought it would likely attract, which, in reality, included almost any man in the area.

Effrontery often began on the overcrowded ships sailing up the coast. Martha Purdy had booked a stateroom with three berths. When she walked in, she saw others' bags on the floor. Obviously, some mistake had been made. "I was soon told that I was to have company," Martha recounted. "The double lower had been allotted to a tinhorn gambler and his female companion, the middle to me and the upper to 'Birdie,' destined to be one of the most notorious characters of the Klondyke. My brother George and I protested to the captain and purser, but . . . in the language of today, 'we could take it or leave it.'" Martha took it.

Less than two years after arriving in Dawson City, working first as a merchant, then as a restaurant operator and later as the owner of two hotels, Belinda Mulrooney had become one of the best-known entrepreneurs in the North. She agreed to accept donations for the city's most prestigious fundraising event, a benefit for St. Mary's Hospital. The town's dance-hall girls and prostitutes, who were as likely to be hospitalized as anyone, wanted to contribute. The money was collected and then given to Belinda's friend and Chilkoot trailmate, Joe Barrette.

"Good God, Joe!" Belinda exclaimed when he told her who had contributed the donation. "What will I do with this? I can't account for this." She told Joe he had better give the donation back, explaining, "They'll think it's dirty money."

Joe took the comment literally and decided to "get all gold dust. That's clean enough."

Belinda shook her head. "It's not that. It's where it comes from. You take it back."

"No, I can't do that," Joe argued. "Fine women! Give to churches! Good as anyone! I know it! You know it. Make the rest know it."

Belinda accepted the donation and labelled it a gift. "That was all the information they could get out of Joe or me," Belinda added. The gift was worth $20,000.

In the Klondike, the mixing and mingling of the classes was short-lived. Within months of its founding, Dawson City began to develop its own social hierarchy. The re-establishment of a familiar social ladder—judges and civil servants on the top rung, prostitutes on the bottom rung—was comforting to most newcomers, who never really felt at ease in the company of any other than "their own kind." Still, after well-established social barriers were broken, many women were never the same again.

"Polly, what will people think of you if you talk like that when we get home?" whined Martha Purdy's brother, George, when he heard her rough, gold-creek language.

"Think of me?" Martha scoffed. "If I get my half-million I won't give a damn," she retorted, still hopeful that she would find the long-lost fortune she had come to the Klondike to locate. "And if I don't," she continued hotly, "then they won't give a damn for me!"

7

A Wife's Duty

FOLLOWING NEWS OF BIG STRIKES in the Klondike, husbands and wives throughout North America argued about whether or not they should try their luck in the North. Should the husband go to the Klondike or simply keep his job and carry on? If he went, should the wife go, too? In the face of this madness, they had to determine what a wife's real duty was: to stay at home with the children or to support her husband on the trails.

Only 3 percent of the 28,000 stampeders who journeyed to the Yukon were women, which suggests that that most wives agreed to stay behind and carry on alone. A few men managed to persuade their wives to accompany them on what many regarded as the grandest adventure of all. Some wives persuaded their husbands to let them tag along, saying the men would not, or could not, go alone. Ethel Berry told a reporter, "I went because my husband went and I wanted to be with him."

Till Death (and Klondike) Do Us Part

Wives and mothers who decided "Ho, for the Klondike" also had to decide if their children should join the trek. For many, the answer was an agonizing "no."

"My sweet, darling Kidlets," one bereft mother wrote from Dawson to her children in far-off New York City. "Being apart from you . . . is the greatest trial I have to endure, and I try very hard to keep from thinking of home and sometimes a few days pass away and I do not look at [the photo of] your sweet faces, because I know my courage and endurance give way . . . I do not think I will write very much more," she closed the letter, "as the tears blind me."

Few couples travelled with their young children, and some wished they hadn't. At least three children were buried on the Chilkoot Trail: one at Dyea and two at Lindeman Lake. Children were particularly susceptible to the hepatitis, meningitis and typhoid that ravaged the trails and Klondike settlements during the gold rush.

Not long after she and George had built a log cabin across the Klondike River from Dawson City, Martha Purdy made a shocking discovery. Her estranged husband, Will, had given her a going-away gift. She was pregnant.

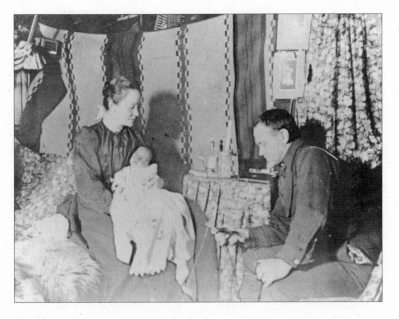

Martha Purdy, her brother George and the little "cheechako" (meaning "tenderfoot") in the cabin above Lousetown.

"I could not believe it. I would not let my mind dwell upon it," she admitted later. "Terror-stricken, I faced this Gethsemane." Martha knew her condition would not allow her to face the long trail to the coast again. There was no getting out now. That fact only accentuated her feeling that she had lost control of her life; she was trapped. "Oh, God," she prayed, "let me die."

"I should never have consented to your coming," George confessed, as the hopelessness of the situation threatened to overwhelm him as well.

Witnessing George's despondency seemed to shake Martha out of her depression. "I determined I would not brood over my troubles. I would not be downed."

She sought help. Father William Judge, the so-called Saint of Dawson and founder of St. Mary's Hospital, told the impoverished mother-to-be it would cost $1,000 to deliver her baby, a sum that was more than the average annual pay at the time. Judge was an aggressive fundraiser, and perhaps he knew Martha came from a wealthy family. He even offered to wait until spring for payment. Instead, Martha decided to deliver the child on her own.

"The baby came ahead of time. I was alone and it was over quickly—an incredibly easy birth—Mother Nature's gift to women who live a natural, out-of-door life such as I had done," Martha later recounted. "And weren't the men-folk surprised when they returned from work at night, to find, wrapped in red flannel—a fine, healthy baby boy!" Martha remembered proudly. "They called him the little cheechako." Martha named the boy Lyman, after her grand-father. Soon, Martha realized that even the men on the trail missed their children back home. "What a welcome the camp gave my baby! The men in our party, and my neigh-bours, all men, took full charge. They kept the fires going. They brought in foodstuffs—fresh-baked bread, cakes, chocolates, ptarmigan, moose meat, every wild delicacy of the country. Miners, prospectors, strange uncouth men called to pay their respects."

A Wife's Duty

During their first few weeks in the Klondike, newlyweds Ethel and Clarence Berry made their meagre home in Fortymile. There was no gold to be found in the muddy tracks between the stores, warehouses and saloons of the little village. So, not long after they had arrived, Clarence left again for the creeks. Ethel was alone in a dismal little log settlement full of rough-and-ready strangers. She had never been alone before. "There was nothing, absolutely nothing to do," she discovered to her dismay. "Just imagine sitting for hours in one's home doing nothing, looking out a scrap of window and seeing nothing, searching for work and finding nothing." Ethel was reduced to walking to a nearby cemetery "for consolation."

Soon, however, Clarence was back in Fortymile. He'd found no gold and had eaten through his outfit. The couple was broke. Actually, their financial distress was a blessing in disguise, because it put cash-strapped Clarence behind the bar of Bill McPhee's saloon. He was on duty, pouring drinks and washing glasses, the fateful night that George Carmack strutted in with his incredible tale of a huge strike. Others were skeptical, but within an hour, Clarence had arranged a grubstake with Bill McPhee and dashed off to tell his wife the news. Before morning, he was rowing upriver, determined to be among the first to stake a claim along the creek.

Ethel played a critical role in Clarence's plan. Having registered his claim at Fort Constantine, the nearby NWMP post, Clarence returned to Fortymile. He threw into his rowboat as many supplies as it would carry, telling Ethel to bring the rest on the next available paddlewheeler. He dashed off again. When the little steamer *Alice* nudged against the bank a few days later, Ethel was informed she had 12 hours to get her supplies together for loading. She put together about five tons of supplies before the appointed departure time. Before the year was out, the Berrys would be millionaires. But their happily-ever-after story was the exception rather than the rule.

The horrific conditions and unremitting exhaustion were enough to end hundreds of partnerships between men. Trying conditions proved equally destructive to marital relationships, as well.

Not long after 1898's spring breakup, 1,000 vessels lay becalmed on Lake Laberge. Suddenly, there was an unexpected gust of wind. Sails snapped and fluttered, and boats jerked this way and that. A woman standing in the stern of one particular scow lost her balance and tumbled into the chilly waters. One of the two men on board raced to the centre of the scow to lower the sail, expecting the other man—the woman's husband—to dive overboard and come to her aid. Instead, the husband panicked and began racing about frantically, screaming for help.

Two prospectors in a nearby boat witnessed the mishap. The steersman dropped his tiller and dived to the woman's rescue. He quickly assisted her to his boat, and with the help of his partner brought her aboard. The scow, meanwhile, had drifted some distance away, so the rescuers rowed over, reuniting the woman with her husband. To their astonishment, the woman announced to her husband and to everyone within earshot that she had all of *him* she wanted. She turned and pointed a finger at her shivering rescuer. "If this man will take me, he can have me," she shouted. The steersman knew a good thing when he saw it.

"Yes, I'll take you," he shouted back.

The steersman's companion wasn't so sure he liked the idea of an unexpected third partner, even one as comely as the woman in question. He made his feelings clear. The rescuer dove under the boat's canvas for his outfit, re-emerged with a six-gun, and levelled it at his wide-eyed partner. The woman was under his protection, he stated. Then, without taking his eyes off his partner, he shouted to the woman's devastated husband to throw her belongings into their boat. The woman reportedly got a divorce from the panicky husband and married her rescuer, to the admiration of everyone who witnessed the incident.

Keeping the Home Fires Burning

Conditions in the Klondike were different in almost every respect from those on the outside. Nevertheless, the traditional roles of men and women were maintained. The brutally tough work that engaged the men on the creeks helped ensure that their wives remained back at the cabin, attending to domestic duties. Men simply didn't have the time or energy for anything other than digging, hauling and sluicing.

Most women were stunned by the paucity of food items available. After Martha Purdy finished making her rude, one-room log house a home, she set about keeping house for George and became hostess to many of his working companions.

"Much against the will of the party," she remembered, she had carried into the Yukon "two linen tablecloths, with two dozen napkins, silver knives, forks and spoons for company." She discovered that food shortages and outrageous prices made for a meagre Klondike larder. "For six months we were to be entirely without butter, sugar or milk," Martha recalled. "Our breakfast consisted of cornmeal mush with molasses and clear coffee. How I longed for a change of diet— some fruit and vegetables!"

There were hundreds of other shortages as well. The midnight sun was a blessing in the summer, but the near-endless dark of winter was a dreadful curse for those who could not afford artificial light. Martha remembered, "After the supper dishes were done, if I sewed, as a special favour, I was allowed two candles."

In the spring of 1898, Tot Bush, Ethel Berry's teenaged sister, joined Ethel and others in the family on their return trip to Klondike. Tot's introduction to the domestic drudgery that she would experience in Eldorado Creek began on the Chilkoot Trail itself. There was scarcely a sign of the huge wealth the Berrys were bringing up from the dirty depths below.

"It was hard work cooking for so many with the same kind of food every day and so few utensils," Tot wrote later of her time in Sheep Camp. "Ethel and I did the cooking for our crowd. We had to set up everything twice for each meal, as we didn't have enough dishes." However, she added proudly, "the cooking smelt so good to strangers passing the tent that they would poke their heads in to ask if it was a boarding house."

A year earlier, in the crazy summer of 1897, when Ethel and Clarence had returned to civilization from Eldorado Creek, they had been besieged by the press. The Berrys fled Seattle and headed to San Francisco, where they were finally interviewed. None of the wives on the creeks described their homemaking challenges better than Ethel. She told *San Francisco Examiner* readers, "We could not get one drop of water without first melting the ice, which necessitated keeping a fire all day. Keeping the fire is enough to occupy the whole of one person's time. The wood is full of pitch and blazes up and is out again almost before one can walk across the room and back." Provisions were often kept in caches, small elevated log enclosures located outside the cabin. This crude food preservation system presented another problem for Ethel: "All our supplies which we kept in the cache had to go through the same process of thawing before being cooked."

Author A.C. Harris wanted to know what the ladies of the Klondike did for fun. He got an earful. "We never felt like playing games or going in for any kind of amusements after the day's hard work was done," Ethel told Harris. "We did not think of anything but sleep and rest. That was the main reason we did not die of homesickness. We had no time to think!"

A reporter asked Ethel if she had advice to give women headed for the Klondike. Ethel replied without hesitation, "Oh, stay away, of course!" Many female newspaper readers undoubtedly heeded her words and abandoned any plans they may have had to go north. Many others who braved the trails and the trials of the Yukon fervently wished they had done the same.

8

Making Their Way

AS ETHEL BERRY AND HER sister discovered, "women's work" began even before reaching the Klondike. Della Banks and her prospector husband, Thompson, were among the first wave of gold seekers to hit the trail in 1897. It wasn't the first time Della had accompanied Thompson on his "perennial search for fortune," so she knew what to expect. Like Emily Craig, Della Banks realized cooking along the trail would fall to her. What was different for Della was that her husband and his companions agreed to pay her for the work. However, she found the money barely compensated for the working conditions.

"I got supper in the rain by the light of a candle," she related over 40 years later. The memories of it all still rankled. "Kneeling on the ground, I mixed biscuits—90 of them, baked fifteen at a time in the sheet-iron stove. Thompson watched, saying that if he had to get supper that night, there wouldn't be any. Well," Della snorted, "I had walked as far as he had."

After surviving the arduous journey to the land of the midnight sun, work began in earnest. Many women had come to the Klondike in search of financial freedom and independence. For those who expected to dig up gold and go home rich, the first few days in Dawson City and on the creeks were a painful shock. Even for 1897's first arrivals, there were few claims left to stake.

For most, finding work—at least, legitimate work away from Paradise Alley—proved almost impossible. However, for those who could overcome the fear and fatigue, there were opportunities waiting.

Cashing in on the Masculine Market

Soon after tents were raised along Dawson City's riverbank, women found financial success, opening businesses such as restaurants, laundries and baths, where many men parted with their gold in return for goods and services.

Anna DeGraf hefted a sewing machine across the Chilkoot more than once. She never lacked work, sewing furs for Jack McQuesten's A.C. Company in Circle City and then, during Dawson's heyday, sewing costumes for the dance-hall girls at the Orpheum Theatre. She also created cold-weather clothes for the NWMP. At one time, Anna employed at least four other women in her workshop. The widow was far too busy to contemplate marriage, although she received at least two proposals. Anna was also successful at staking many claims. She received numerous tips about open claims and would stealthily wander up the creeks in the dead of night to hammer in her stakes before competitors arrived at dawn.

Having left Seattle, Frances Dorley was determined to stay in the North. After three months of searching, she found a cabin near Grand Forks, at the junction of Bonanza and Eldorado creeks. She converted the building into a roadhouse for weary travellers. "I baked tons of bread and pies and made millions of doughnuts," she recalled. Butter arrived in five-pound wooden buckets. Once emptied of butter, Frances filled them with baked beans.

By spring, Frances was back in Dawson City and had reacquainted herself with a certain Mrs. Moore, a middle-aged southern widow she had met at Lake Bennett the year before. The two women entered a partnership, and their Professional Men's Boarding House became a rip-roaring success.

As she had done in so many other gold camps, Nellie Cashman turned to food service for income and opened Dawson's Can-Can in the early summer of 1898. By the fall, she had opened the Cassiar Restaurant and had also operated a store. Cashman's lasting fame came from her philanthropy. Her legendary generosity began years earlier in BC, where she provided tender care to prospectors who gave her the nickname "Angel of the Cassiar." A few weeks after arriving in the Klondike, Nellie was walking the creeks, asking prospectors to dig deep for an expansion to St. Mary's Hospital.

A tender-hearted woman, Nellie looked and sounded like a tough-talking gold-field veteran. Her relationship with prospectors was unique. "Men are a nuisance," she complained good-naturedly to an interviewer. "Men— why, child, they're just boys grown up. I've nursed them, embalmed them, fed and scolded them, acted as mother confessor and fought my own with them and you have to treat them just like boys."

Kate Ryan was perhaps the best-known restaurateur on the Stikine Trail. Initially, the former nurse fed members of the NWMP and later opened a Glenora restaurant. After two years of travel, Kate arrived in Canada's newest railway town, Whitehorse, where she opened Kate's Café. Here, her life turned in an unusual direction.

Soon after her arrival, the NWMP called on Kate to take a job as prison matron. Gold smuggling had become a concern, and the Canadian government required a female gold inspector. Formidable-looking Kate was the only serious candidate for the position. She accepted a post as woman special constable, designed her own uniform and began riding the trains and the steamers, asking passengers if they had any gold to declare.

On board a steamer docked at Whitehorse, Constable

Ryan's question was greeted by indignant silence from one fashionable woman. Kate repeated the question, but to no avail. "I'm sorry, madam, but if you do not answer the questions, you will have to be searched."

"Oh, scarcely," came the haughty reply. "Do you know to whom you are speaking? I am the wife of Major General Gerald Brompton of the United States Army."

"And I, madam, am myself an officer of the British Crown. Would you kindly step into the cabin?"

Moments later, the woman had literally let down her hair, reluctantly exposing a number of concealed nuggets.

There were big profits to be made on Dawson City's seamy side. Within four months of her arrival from the Australian gold fields, unorthodox Marguerite Laimee opened the first of two Dawson cigar stores, which were merely fronts for bawdy houses. Traffic was so good that she poured $30 of gold into her pokes each morning from floor sweepings. The "stores" grossed $60,000 in less than two years. With the profits, Marguerite purchased a prime half-acre city lot for just $750 and quickly leased it for $500 a month. But her biggest financial windfall was yet to come.

Women of the Creeks

The few women who made their way north to the confluence of the Yukon and Klondike rivers shared the fate of most male stampeders: they were too late to stake claims. Those who did become prospectors either purchased claims from others or invested in a share of working prospects. Most of these women had much more profitable—and less contentious—sources of revenue.

Nellie Cashman invested her restaurant returns in claims, but was soon beset with legal disputes. The most serious allegation was that Nellie had tried to bribe Belinda Mulrooney by threatening to reveal information about Belinda's business associations with the mining inspector. Commissioner William Ogilvie was forced to investigate, and Nellie confessed she had been in error. Her obvious record of community work stood her in good stead, and no charges were laid.

Nellie struck it big with 19 below (the first, or "discovery" claim) on Bonanza Creek. She eventually bought out her partners and carted away more than $100,000 of ore. The proceeds bought her some less profitable claims, which she travelled to on snowshoes or by her dog team.

By the spring of 1899, Martha Purdy had managed to stake some claims on lesser-known Excelsior Creek. Within a few months, the claims were worth tens of thousands of dollars, and Martha, her brother and two partners were employing a crew of 16 to work them. She not only managed the businesses, but their kitchen too, cooking for all the men.

By 1901, Martha's family moved north to the Klondike from the US. They brought to Dawson the latest in mining technology—a mill to process ore and a hydraulic "monitor," and equipment to start a sawmill. The monitor's high-pressure jets of water left no gold concealed on Martha's holdings at her original mining claims. Soon, business was booming at the sawmill as well; money was rolling in, but success brought problems.

Martha took over lumber marketing after firing her salesman because of drunkenness. By the following spring, the sawmill foreman decided that he "wasn't gonna be run by a skirt." Equipment was sabotaged and the foreman was the primary suspect. When sabotage failed to stop production, the foreman coerced the men to pull out and incited the workers to stage a dramatic showdown in Martha's office. Purdy called their bluff, wrote out the men's final cheques and ordered the foreman off the property. When the foreman's public threats against Martha Purdy continued, the Mounties bluntly advised him to leave the Klondike.

"I'll get that hellcat yet!" the malcontent screamed as he shoved off from the wharf. Some days later when he entered American territory, a sheriff, perhaps tipped off by the NWMP, was waiting with a long-standing warrant and took him into custody. Meanwhile, "hellcat" Purdy kept on making "plenty of money," which allowed her to "buy the most beautiful clothes." It had been a long, hard struggle—"tough sledding," she called it—since her days as a separated pregnant mother struggling up the Trail of '98.

For legal advice, Martha turned to fellow Klondiker

and lawyer George Black. In the course of conversation, the lawyer mentioned that he was interested in becoming a politician and also suggested he was interested in something else—marriage to Martha. Two weeks after that initial legal consultation, George Black proposed. Martha admitted there was much to recommend the match (George Black and her boys hit it off almost immediately), but perhaps remembering her earlier, ill-fated marriage, Martha stated, "For once in my life, I let my head govern my heart." If George were serious, he would be patient.

It took Martha Purdy two years to accept George's proposal, but when she did, her life changed forever. Decades later, the couple moved to Ottawa. George Black became Speaker of the House of Commons, and later, Martha Black became a Member of Parliament at age 69.

The Klondike Mogul
Within days of her party's arrival in the Klondike, feisty, Irish-born entrepreneur Belinda Mulrooney began to explore retail opportunities in Canada's newest northern settlement. She partnered with three newcomers from Circle City, Alaska: a woman of questionable virtue named Esther Duffie, and two married women who had braved the trek up the icy river to Dawson City.

Belinda had brought long metal cylinders full of silks over the Chilkoot Trail. "I've been a fool," she thought bitterly, fearing that no one would buy delicate silks in such a boom-town environment. Hiding her embarrassment, Belinda opened one of the cylinders. The others greedily fingered the silk garments, and Belinda's doubts about how she would earn an income vanished.

Belinda watched prospectors' Native wives shuffle down the waterfront pathway in mukluks, short skirts and heavy workshirts. They came to the store, dashed away quickly and returned a while later, dragging their grizzled husbands. Esther Duffie would hold up a particularly exquisite item for the couples to view.

"What's that good for?" one miner shouted.

"That'll be a fine outfit when the mosquitoes get after you," laughed another.

Many of the women did not know how to wear the items their men bought. They were happy enough to own such fine fashions and to feel the silk in their hands.

"Next!" Esther would holler. "Who wants a beautiful night dress?"

Clever and beguiling, Esther manipulated the scales weighing the prospectors' gold in a way that made even Belinda blush. Esther might be merely a whore in Circle City, but she was a formidable saleswoman in Dawson. Belinda earned a 600 percent profit on the sale of her goods.

The women wanted silks; the men wanted meals. There was only one problem: a supply shortage. Belinda knew that every man with an outfit was a potential restaurant customer. She proposed an offer few men could refuse. If they gave her their food, they would receive cash or credit at her new restaurant. Most of the men hated cooking, so the restaurant's inventory swelled. In the land of the midnight sun, Belinda's restaurant did a roaring trade 24 hours a day.

With the profits, Belinda bought lots on Front Street, opposite the Yukon River. She dismantled river rafts and turned them into money-making riverfront cabins. After visiting the creeks, Belinda developed an idea that had the miners rolling with mirth: she decided to build a hotel not far from where Bonanza and Eldorado creeks diverged. The laughing stopped when the newly finished, two-storey Grand Forks Hotel quickly filled with tenants. Before long, a town had sprung up around the establishment. Belinda's dream, however, was to build a hotel in Dawson City. She would call the three-storey structure "The Fairview."

Others, including prospector-millionaire Alex McDonald, Belinda's rival and partner, shook their heads. "Alex and . . . Joe Barrette don't want you to try and build that hotel," Grand Forks Hotel manager Walter Gilmer told Belinda. "They don't feel you can make a go of it."

"I guess that's just why I'm going to build it," Belinda answered defiantly. "If they didn't say that, I wouldn't think of it."

Belinda secretly arranged a $10,000 bet that she would finish the hotel. One bet became many. Men even bet she would never be able to heat the building. They hadn't counted on her innovative "central heating" system. A large coal-oil tank was converted into a furnace. Later, she was told that men had put up as much as $100,000.

Build it she did, and she won the bets, too. The hotel was "by far the most prestigious structure now in Dawson," raved the *Nugget*. From Grand Forks, some eight kilometres away, the mining inspector declared the hotel open, making his grand announcement via a new invention called the telephone. There were speeches, food, champagne and dancing to "one perfectly equipped orchestra," as Belinda put it. It was a triumph for the mogul, who was all of 27 years old.

Belinda was more than a visionary. The tenacious woman managed to turn dreams into realities, not only for her own profit, but for the betterment of Dawson. Belinda Mulrooney's energy, influence and cash were behind amenities from hotels and sanitary water systems to telephone and fire services.

The pressure had been relentless throughout the hotel's construction. Belinda had needed building supplies, but time was the enemy. In Skagway, she told packer Joe Brooks it was imperative that he deliver supplies from the port city to Lake Bennett in just three days. He agreed and charged her premium fees for the task. Belinda concluded that if Joe could manage the delivery, it was worth the high price. She raced to Bennett to await the supplies. An employee hurried after Belinda, telling her that Joe Brooks had dumped her supplies at the summit of the pass! Saloon-keeper Bill

McPhee had offered the packer more money to move his whisky to the Bennett steamboats. Belinda was enraged.

Belinda and her employee rode up to the summit, hired a bunch of tough men on the trail and rode down past the NWMP post into American territory. There, they could ambush Joe and his boys without running afoul of Canadian law. As Joe's mule train ambled up, loaded with Bill McPhee's supplies, Belinda trotted into the centre of the trail. She calmly told the foreman she wouldn't budge until he had read one specific clause of her contract with Brooks. The clause stated she could take possession of Joe Brooks' pack-train mules at any time if the conditions of the contract were not met.

"We're not bothered with a contract, woman," the fore-man laughed, "You'll have a hell of a chance taking this pack train."

It seemed like a standoff, but Belinda was prepared. She had every intention of enforcing the clause. "Well, old man," Belinda smiled, urging her horse up to the foreman's, "I hate to do it, but I must." Suddenly, the foreman was looking down at the barrel of Belinda's revolver, which was prodding him painfully beneath his belt. "You better get off," Belinda warned him. The foreman dismounted.

Actually, Belinda felt she was doing the fellow a favour. "I only pulled the gun on him to give him a decent excuse for giving up the mules," she confessed. "A man had to have a decent excuse in Skagway. Of course, my men took the foreman and messed him up enough to make him feel it was a real holdup."

Belinda's gang took the mules, unloaded Bill McPhee's liquor, loaded up her supplies and took the foreman in tow. Then she offered Joe Brooks' men jobs, which they eagerly accepted. "Brooks' crew thought it was all a wonderful joke on him," Belinda recalled. To inflame their former boss even further, the men gave Belinda Joe's horse. "Everyone on the trail knew Brooks' pinto," Belinda laughed later. "Said I might as well have it. That horse was the swellest little animal I ever knew."

In the summer of 1898, at the height of the gold rush, a stocky man of medium height, proud bearing and cultured, perhaps even foppish mannerisms arrived in Dawson City. He was accompanied by a valet, of all things, and the two men immediately booked rooms in the best hotel in town, Mulrooney's Fairview. This was no prospector; this was Charles Eugene Carbonneau. The newcomer told others he was a representative of a French winery. While that may have been true, he wasn't in Dawson to market wine. He was there on behalf of a consortium of English investors to purchase mining claims.

Within days of his arrival, Carbonneau met Belinda Mulrooney. The occasion was less than auspicious: she walked in while he was arguing with her hotel manager about the cost of a bottle of wine. When she offered to pay for it, he reversed his position and insisted on paying for what she called "that darn little bottle" himself. Carbonneau's business card stated he was a count. Belinda was miffed by the title. She had no patience with people who put on airs and let him know it. He hastily snatched the card from her sight.

A French count? Others were doubtful; the rumours began. A claims foreman on the Eldorado thought he remembered Carbonneau as a Montreal barber. One of the owners of the *Klondike Nugget* heard from a man on the trail that Carbonneau had been a Montreal cook. A shocking story from the trail fuelled the rumour mill. Anxious to set a winter travelling record from Skagway to Dawson, the count had whipped his sled team furiously, leaving "dead and dying dogs behind him," the *Seattle Post-Intelligencer* reported. "Half a dozen dogs . . . almost dead from exhaustion, left alone to freeze and starve." No self-respecting sourdough could countenance such heartlessness. Suspicion gave way to animosity.

Belinda Mulrooney wrote off the rumours to petty jealousy. What impressed her more was that Carbonneau was a "dashing sort of chap in his good clothes." She admitted she found his "conversation restful and interesting." And his gifts kept coming.

As the most successful businesswoman in the Klondike (Martha Purdy would make her fortune three years later), Belinda Mulrooney was in a class by herself. Who might she choose as a suitable husband? Certainly not a typical grubby prospector. The question was important; the years were flying by and Belinda Mulrooney wanted children. Her friends suspected as much, just as they also suspected that what Carbonneau wanted was Belinda's money.

Belinda Mulrooney may have had a genius for business, but she was naive about affairs of the heart. After Carbonneau proposed, even the priest advised against the marriage. Some friends refused to attend the ceremony. The wedding went ahead anyway, one of the most lavish nuptials staged in gold-rush Dawson.

As the couple's wealth increased and their mine holdings grew, they spent winters in Paris and summers in the Klondike, and later, in Fairbanks, Alaska, where Belinda founded a bank. However, it was finally obvious even to Belinda that the count loved her money more than he loved her. In 1906, still childless, Belinda divorced Carbonneau. Thirteen years later, after being charged in a railroad swindle, Carbonneau was found dead in his French prison cell.

Belinda Mulrooney retired to Carbonneau Castle, her turreted, two-storey faux-stone home set in 20 acres of Yakima, Washington, orchards. By 1920, her Yukon and Alaska fortunes dwindling away, Belinda was renting the home out to meet expenses. In 1943, the 71-year-old former Klondike mogul donned a hard hat to help build minesweepers for Associated Ship Builders. "Well, why not?" she told an interviewer in her typical, no-nonsense style. "I've really worked all my life and this is certainly no time to be idle. We've got a war to win."

9

Citizens of the Demimonde

LAUNDRY, COOKING, ACCOMMODATION and hot baths weren't the only services women made available to thousands of Klondike gold seekers. For many men, especially those who had been successful on the creeks, "hospitality" services were priority purchases.

Practitioners of "the oldest profession," "citizens of the demimonde," "soiled doves" and "ladies of the tenderloin" were some of the euphemisms polite society and its sniggering newspaper writers used to describe the women who worked as prostitutes. They were part of Yukon culture long before George Carmack and his partners made their enormous strike.

Dancing Across the Line of Decorum

In her biography, Martha (Purdy) Black maintained there were three classes of women in the Klondike: those of "the oldest profession," dance-hall and variety girls and others, including "wives of an unbounded faith in and love for their mate." Martha grouped entertainers with prostitutes, and in doing so reflected the prevailing attitude of the day. In some instances, she may have been correct in her assumption. Nobody knows how many dance-hall girls and entertainers strayed across the line of morality as circumstances dictated. However, as Belinda Mulrooney insisted, some women actually stepped the other way.

"Many who got caught in the mess of the trail changed their names and when they got to Dawson, started to swing men around in the dance hall. Some never took a drink. Maybe you don't know it," Belinda told an interviewer, "but some of the best women in the northwest today have been in those Klondike dance halls."

Despite popular belief, dance-hall girls were not chorus-line women who did high kicks on stages. Instead, they were paid by lonely men simply to dance with them, working the floor between shows, shuffling through more than 100 dances a night. They were also called "percentage girls," because they received a commission on the dollar-a-dance money they earned on the floor or in the theatre boxes, where, as "box-rushers," they enticed men to drink away their rawhide pokes of gold dust.

Ladies of the evening "at work." Behind the group are the notorious cribs, each with enough room for a bed, a chair and a washstand.

A few Klondike entertainers, such as Mae Field and New York stage actress Esther Lyon, alias Cad Wilson, were well received in theatres, saloons and dance halls, as well as in the parlours of polite society. Many made more than $200 a month, much more than Sam Steele's police constables took back to their barracks or many hard-working prospectors wrenched out of the ground. Cad Wilson, whose brilliant fame concealed a mysterious past, was one of the most successful. When she left the Yukon in the summer of 1899, she packed up $26,000 and a huge nugget necklace.

Was Cad Wilson the famous New York stage performer Esther Lyons Robinson? Perhaps. Had Esther accompanied photographer Veazine Wilson on the Chilkoot back in 1894 and returned to the Yukon under a new stage name? Possibly, although the mature-looking newcomer from San Francisco told folks in Dawson City she was just 16 and fresh from a convent in Sacramento. Age aside, the fact that Wilson didn't *look* glamorous lent passing credibility to her story. In fact, in one 1898 photograph, Cad Wilson resembles someone's pleasant middle-aged mother rather than the woman who became the obsession of adoring fans from one end of the Klondike to the other.

Prospector Mont Hawthorne remembered her in his memoir *The Trail Led North*: "She danced so light her feet hardly touched the floor at all. The fellows went mad when she was singing 'There'll be a Hot Time in the Old Town Tonight.' That's when they really began throwing nuggets on the stage. Cad had a laugh that was a little different. She'd sing a while and then she'd look around and laugh. She used her dress for holding nuggets just like it was sort of an apron."

At this performance, Cad was also wearing nuggets. Some prospectors on Eldorado Creek had made her a heavy, ornate belt that "went clean around her once and a half and there wasn't even a medium-sized nugget in the bunch," Hawthorne recalled. She reportedly left the Yukon not only with the belt but with thousands of dollars in cash, drafts for tens of thousands more and, a Chicago newspaper noted, "diamonds of sufficient variety and number to light the entire Great Northern hotel, where she is stopping."

Cad Wilson's repertoire wouldn't raise any eyebrows today, but more than a century ago men were more easily titillated. The mere sight of a woman's ankles was enough to get pulses pounding. Cad's most famous number was a ditty called "Such a Nice Girl, Too," and she shocked Belinda Mulrooney and other ladies attending an Elks Club fundraiser by singing:

> Last week they took her up to court,
> She said, 'Judge do be forgiving,'
> He answered, 'yes, if you can prove
> You've not three husbands living.

When the news of Nome's gold strikes spirited close to 8,000 prospectors out of Dawson City in one fateful week in 1900, Cad Wilson went with them, entertaining the Alaska gold seekers on the Bering Sea for a few undoubtedly profitable months before disappearing from the footlights and history forever.

Stage entertainers and dance-hall girls often stepped back and forth over the invisible line between legitimate work and prostitution whenever it was worth their while to do so. One of the most infamous dance-hall girls who worked both sides was Mae Field. Mae was just 17 and already a dancer when she married Arthur Field early in 1898 in South Dakota. Somehow, the couple heard about the early gold finds in the Yukon and arrived in Dawson City a month before the arrival of the *Excelsior* in San Francisco ignited the rush. Mae and Arthur managed to accomplish what most stampeders who followed them could only dream of doing: they made a gold strike worth $100,000.

However, lady luck turned fickle. Arthur invested badly, lost almost everything and the two "drifted apart." Fortunately, Mae was able to return to her talents as a dancer. Before long, she was a headlining the Flora Dora Dance Hall as "The Doll of Dawson." Mae Field quickly became one of the city's most popular performers. Five years later, she was still before the footlights, six nights a week, at the Orpheum Theatre, making more than most of the city's entertainers. However, her fame and not inconsiderable earnings obviously did not provide the personal satisfaction Mae craved.

In 1903, under the headline SUICIDE, the *Klondike Nugget* informed its readers that, tired "of the joys of living," Mae had walked into a saloon, shot herself in the head "with poor effect" (the bullet passed through her hair) and was duly arrested. She was given a suspended sentence, but a few months later she was before the judge again, the defendant in an assault suit brought by a woman who appeared swathed in bandages.

It's likely the lure of prostitution's easy money proved too great for Mae to resist, and the following year, described by a licence inspector as a "well-known notorious character about town," Mae set herself and another woman up in the Royal Hotel. When the "Lewd woman" and her female companion were tossed out of her rooms, she bought a house and two cabins a few steps from the police station, hung out a sign reading "Furnished Rooms" and welcomed all comers. Unbeknownst to Mae, her house was under police surveillance.

When their loud knocking went unheeded early one morning, NWMP officers broke into the house and caught Mae in bed with an unmarried man. In 1908, that was enough to sentence a woman of Mae's reputation to six months' hard labour and an order to leave the country. Mae served her sentence and packed up. By 1912, she was living in Ketchikan, Alaska, the proprietor of a respectable boarding house.

Mae kept her shady past a secret for decades. "People didn't ask personal questions in the north," an elderly Mae Field told a freelance magazine writer in the 1940s. "Not in those days."

It appears Mae chose prostitution as an easy way to make additional cash, but others turned to the world's oldest profession out of desperation. One unfortunate was a young Seattle woman the *Klondike Nugget* dubbed Milley Lane. "That is not her name; we cannot advertise these people," the newspaper sniffed, ignoring a more compassionate reason for the pseudonym: protecting the true identity of the unfortunate woman. Destitute and hungry after three fruitless days of job-hunting, Milley had but two choices, the newspaper maintained: "Jump into the river or go to board with one of the madams in Dawson's Whitechapel." Whitechapel was the newspaper's ill-conceived attempt at a parallel with the notorious low-life district of London, England. Milley's trail acquaintances, who hadn't given the girl a hand up or even a handout, professed shock that the woman chose "the madams."

As Belinda Mulrooney's long-time employee, Esther Duffie was more fortunate than most. Belinda proved to be a broad-minded, practical employer. After the Front Street tent store folded, Esther found work in Belinda's restaurant and was one of the kitchen crew at the Fairview Hotel's grand opening celebration. A few weeks later, more to appease the righteous than for any other reason, the NWMP staged a rare, well-publicized tenderloin raid. They rounded up 69 of the soiled doves, including Esther Duffie. Belinda, who "never lost respect and liking" for Esther, offered forgiveness, choosing to ignore her friend's carousing lifestyle, saying, "Both my eyes were shut when she went on a spree." Esther eventually journeyed to Alaska with Belinda to be part of the gold-rush excitement in Fairbanks.

Like all other Klondikers, prostitutes came from around the globe, from as far away as Sweden, Germany, France and Japan. Martha Black recalled a group from Belgium that arrived in 1898. The women offered their services in Dawson City, Lousetown and Grand Forks.

Wherever they worked, most prostitutes lived in poverty.

When a prospector walked out of the crib, typically after about 15 minutes, he usually left behind about eight ounces of gold dust, worth about $128. There was little of it left for the women to spend after their pimps, madams or landlords came to collect. The Klondike's high prices quickly emptied their purses of what remained. During freeze-up, claimholders could not wash gold from the creeks, and their incomes suffered. In preparation for pending hardships, Mabel Larose auctioned herself off for the winter in the Monte Carlo Saloon. When the bidding was done, Mabel had fetched room, board and $5,000 in exchange for her exclusive services. She likely was the envy of many of her colleagues.

Life and Death on the Wrong Side of Town

Life was difficult for almost everyone during the gold rush, but women living in Dawson's tenderloin districts faced unthinkable risks.

As bystanders in a Dawson City alley carried a gunshot victim, Mrs. La Ghrist, to the Good Samaritan Hospital, NWMP officers elbowed their way into her shack. They discovered the woman's husband, John La Ghrist, lying jammed between the door and a wall, a bullet hole in his temple.

The La Ghrist shooting was Dawson City's third sordid murder-suicide attempt during the three gold-rush years. The first two women died with their murderous men. John La Ghrist was less successful than his predecessors. Despite receiving three gunshot wounds, his estranged wife survived. The only fatal shot he managed to fire was the one directed at his own head.

Anna DeGraf, a gifted seamstress, worked closely with prostitutes and their abusers in Juneau, Circle City and Dawson City. Anna knew the dangers "women of the mean streets" faced and assisted them beyond simply sewing their gowns. Anna quickly earned a reputation as a feisty, no-nonsense woman after she smashed a would-be thief across the face with a log from her fireside woodpile.

One night, Anna recalled years later, a dance-hall girl burst into her home, begging for help and "groaning and suffering terribly." Six men had broken into the dancer's cabin and attempted to rape her. Shoved up against her cookstove by men desperate to stop her struggles and make her submit, the woman had been badly burned.

"Don't let them get me," the woman pleaded.

Anna put her to bed, told her to be quiet, turned out the light and then "stood with my sixshooter and waited." She did not have to wait long. She could hear the men—"like a pack of wolves!"—outside her cabin. Then came the dreaded knock at her door.

"We want the woman in your cabin," a voice demanded. "We won't bother you if you let us have her."

"You won't get her as long as I am in here with my gun," Anna shouted back.

Members of the unseen mob began to rattle and shake

the door. Anna counted to three and let loose with the revolver. She sent three shots through the door, "And then I heard them run."

During the time she lived and worked in Dawson, Anna delivered matching blue dresses to a pair of dancers. Upon Anna's arrival at the women's hotel room, one of the dancers immediately burst into tears. She led Anna to her roommate, a little blonde "so beautiful and fair—but now so cold and still."

The girl was dead. Her lover had become interested in another woman. In a fit of jealousy, the dancer had taken her own life. While Anna and the distraught dance-hall girl stood by the bed, the lover arrived. Anna watched as he casually looked at the tragic scene, lit a cigarette and calmly walked out of the room.

"Oh, what men," Anna thought in disgust, but that very night "another girl took her place, wore her costume—life went on the same, and nobody bothered about her."

Making the Most of it All

Not all prostitutes and dance-hall girls were innocent, big-hearted victims. Some of them were paid to take advantage of the men they enticed. These talents came naturally to women who schemed beyond professional fleecing in saloons and dance halls.

Juneau's "Queen of Burlesque," 20-year-old Violet Raymond, arrived in Dawson City when tents still lined the riverbank. She and others in an entertainment troupe opened the log-built, two-storey Opera House. Violet's Klondike career lasted just four weeks. During that time, she met and charmed Clarence Berry's partner, Anton Stander, one of the wealthiest Eldorado Creek claimholders. When Violet and Anton left the Yukon, $75,000 of the prospector's $200,000 haul was already in Violet's name. Anton's jealous, drunken rages soon sent the former entertainer packing. Anton died a pauper, as much a victim of alcohol and worthless future mining claims as Violet's avarice. However, when Violet passed away in 1944, her estate was worth $50,000, a sizeable fortune in the days when the average annual salary was less than $1,200.

Nineteen-year-old Gussie Lamore enchanted diminutive "Swiftwater" Bill Gates, another wealthy claimholder who left a large poke of gold dust lying at her feet and a marriage proposal ringing in her ears. She accepted his invitation and swindled him out of a small fortune before blithely stepping onto a steamer bound for San Francisco. "He was too easy— the easiest thing you ever saw," she confessed to the *Seattle Daily Times*. "All you had to do was touch him for $500 and get it. But I wouldn't have married him for all the gold in the Klondike."

Monte Carlo entertainer Grace Drummond left her husband, Edgar Mizner, after the pompous merchant lost nearly $20,000 in one night of reckless roulette play. Grace promised to move in with another Klondike millionaire, Charlie "Lucky Swede" Anderson, if he would put $50,000 in her bank account. Charlie, who had drunkenly purchased what became one of the Klondike's richest claims, quickly agreed. The happy couple toured Europe before returning to San Francisco, where they built a mansion and invested in real estate. Unfortunately, the San Francisco earthquake levelled their investments. Before long, Grace and the fortune were gone, and Charlie ended his life working as a labourer in a BC sawmill.

Dawson cigar-store operator Marguerite Laimee reaped the rewards of the Klondike's biggest matrimonial payoff. The "business woman" was a guest at a lavish dinner at one of the city's hotels when she noticed a good-looking gent across the room. Marguerite had not recognized his face, but she certainly recognized his name: George Carmack, the man whose Bonanza Creek strike had started the world's greatest gold rush.

Marguerite's timing was perfect. George had just returned from the outside, beset with professional and personal problems. Attractive, 26-year-old Marguerite so bedazzled George that he asked her to marry him before the night was done. Marguerite didn't hesitate to accept. She promised to sell her Dawson properties and settle with him in Seattle. Less than two weeks later, George and Marguerite boarded a train to Skagway, never to return to the North.

For many years, life was good for the Carmacks. Real estate properties brought them riches. After George died of pneumonia, his daughter and sister sued Marguerite for the estate. When the dust settled and the legal wrangling was over, Marguerite was still a wealthy woman. However, mining prospects she had purchased with the remains of George's Klondike fortune proved worthless. When she died in 1942, Marguerite lived in a modest house, having lost millions of dollars.

Of all the entertainers, dance-hall girls and prostitutes, only one enjoyed long-lasting notoriety in the decades that followed. Even though Kate Rockwell arrived in Dawson at the end of the rush, over time she came to personify the Klondike's heyday. Kate managed to wring more public relations value out of her two brief years in the Yukon than any other person, enjoying appearances in Hollywood, in the press, on radio and even on television. Single-handedly, Kate kept the rags-to-riches lure of the Klondike alive and would eventually turn tragedy into a personal triumph.

From all accounts, Kate's dance-hall performances were spectacular, and she became a Dawson City sensation. However, for the woman who inscribed her photos "Mush on and smile," it was as much her warm personality as her performances that won the hearts of thousands of men. One day in 1900, she noticed a handsome, swarthy waiter working at the Savoy. His name was Alexander Pantages.

Ambitious and creative, Alexander envisioned owning a chain of theatres, and before long, Kate became part of his plan. Kate's talent had already guaranteed her own wealth, and based on Pantages' promise of marriage, she began to bankroll the now-jobless waiter's first venture, the Orpheum

Unlike many Dawson dance-hall girls and
prostitutes, Kate "Kitty" Rockwell possessed
a classic beauty that captivated thousands
of men.

Theatre, where Mae Field was later to star. Later in Seattle, as
the theatre chain began to take shape, Alex married someone else. Kate's 1905 breach-of-promise suit brought her less
than $5,000.

From time to time, Kate tapped Alexander for money,
and the nervous millionaire paid, fearful that this still-lovely
ghost from his past might injure his reputation. In 1929, a

17-year-old dancer charged the theatre mogul with assault and rape. Kate, the self-styled "Queen of the Yukon," received a subpoena from the district attorney's office. Her world was never the same again.

When the guilty verdict was read, Kate's heartbreaking story was splashed over the front page of the Los Angeles *Evening Herald*. Photographs showed her clenching a hand-kerchief, dabbing at non-existent tears. Kate received amazing media coverage, considering she never took the stand. "I never testified against Alexander Pantages," she said, taking full credit for her absence of testimony, "because win or lose, a sourdough never squeals."

The notoriety made her both a celebrity and a legend. Two years later, Kate married Johnny Matson, a real-life sourdough who had fallen in love with her after seeing her perform in Dawson City some 30 years earlier. The old prospector was still wandering the Yukon, looking for the motherlode. Their Vancouver wedding made international news, and Kate became the subject of numerous interviews. She took a turn as parade marshal, participated in ribbon cuttings and finally received an on-screen credit as Hollywood technical advisor to the producers of the 1944 B movie *Klondike Kate*, starring Ann Savage.

"Entirely fictional," she sniffed. In hotel lobbies and high-class restaurants, she would hike up her skirt to show off her still-shapely legs and demonstrate how she "rolled her own" for a really satisfying sourdough smoke.

"If I had my life to live over, I wouldn't do it much differently," she said proudly. "I've done a lot of living since the days when I was a girl with flaming red hair and twinkling feet. I've had fame and fortune, joy and heartbreak, but I wouldn't change a minute of it."

Many other gold-rush women felt much the same way. Over time, the trials and tribulations so many women suffered seemed somehow trivial. Contentment and satisfaction came from the wild, untamed land as much as anything else.

"It takes the solitude of frozen nights with the howl of dogs for company, the glistening fairness of days when nature reaches out and loves you, she's so beautiful, to bring out the soul in folks," Nellie Cashman maintained. "Banging trolley cars, honking cars, clubs for catty women and false standards of living won't do it."

"You just feast on it," Belinda Mulrooney said of the Yukon. "You become quite religious, seem to get inspiration. Or it might be the electricity in the air. You are filled with it, ready to go."

"I could not shake off the lure of the Klondike," Martha Black admitted, recalling how unhappy she had been while visiting her parents in Kansas for a brief period in 1899. "My thoughts were continually of that vast new, rugged country, its stark and splendid mountains, its lordly Yukon River."

Unknowingly speaking for the hundreds of women who left their world behind, Martha added, "What I wanted was not shelter and safety, but liberty and opportunity."

Bibliography

Backhouse, Frances. *Women of the Klondike*. Vancouver: Whitecap Books, 2002.

Berton, Pierre. *Klondike: The Last Great Gold Rush 1896–1899*. Rev. ed. Toronto: McClelland & Stewart Ltd., 1975.

Black, Martha Louise. *My Ninety Years*. Anchorage: Alaska Northwest Publishing Company, 1976.

Brennan, T. Ann. *The Real Klondike Kate*. Fredericton: Goose Lane Editions, 1990.

Bronson, William. *The Last Grand Adventure*. New York: McGraw-Hill Book Company, 1977.

Duncan, Jennifer. *Frontier Spirit: The Brave Women of the Klondike*. Toronto: Anchor Canada, 2004.

Greenhous, Brereton, ed. *Guarding the Gold Fields: The Story of the Yukon Field Force*. Toronto: Dundurn Press Ltd., 1987.

Johnson, James Albert. *George Carmack*. Vancouver: Whitecap Books, 2001.

Laurence, Frances. *Maverick Women*. Carpinteria, CA: Manifest Publications, 1998.

Lucia, Ellis. *Klondike Kate*. New York: Hastings House Publishers, 1962.

Mayer, Melanie J. *Klondike Women: True Tales of the 1897–1898 Gold Rush*. Athens, Ohio: Swallow Press, 1989.

Mayer, Melanie J. *Staking Her Claim: The Life of Belinda Mulrooney*. Athens, Ohio: Swallow Press, 2000.

Morgan, Lael. *Good Time Girls of the Alaska-Yukon Gold Rush.* Vancouver: Whitecap Books, 1998.

Moynahan, Jay. *Red Light Revelations.* Spokane: Chickadee Publishing, 2001.

Murphy, Claire Rudolf and Jane G. Haigh, *Gold Rush Women.* Anchorage: Alaska Northwest Books, 1997.

O'Connor, Richard. *High Jinks on the Klondike.* New York: Bobbs-Merrill Company Ltd., 1954.

Porsild, Charlene. *Gamblers and Dreamers.* Vancouver: UBC Press, 1998.

Steele, Samuel B. *Forty Years in Canada.* New York: Dodd, Mead & Co., 1915. Reprint, Toronto: Prospero Books, 2000.

Walden, Arthur T. *A Dog Puncher on the Yukon.* Boston: Houghton Mifflin Co., 1928. Reprint, Whitehorse: Wolf Creek Books, 2001.

Index

141

Acknowledgements

I owe a debt of gratitude to many writers whose works helped make this book possible. Chief among them is professor emerita of the University of California Melanie J. Mayer. Mayer's *Klondike Women* does much to shed light on the life and times of the "fairer sex" in the Klondike. Her biography of Belinda Mulrooney, *Staking Her Claim*, co-authored with noted Alaska historian Robert DeArmond, provides a comprehensive account of one of the wealthiest women in the Klondike and many fascinating glimpses of Dawson City, Grand Forks and the people who inhabited the Klondike during the gold rush.

Four Canadian books provided invaluable material for this volume. Martha Louise Black's *My Ninety Years* is among the best eye-witness accounts of the Klondike Gold Rush era. T. Ann Brennan's *The Real Klondike Kate* and Brereton Greenhous' *Guarding the Goldfields* provided accounts of travels on the Stikine Trail. Two comprehensive overviews, Frances Backhouse's *Women of the Klondike* and Jennifer Duncan's more recent *Frontier Spirit*, provided a wealth of detail on the amazing experiences of many rebel women of the Klondike.

Sadly, very few first-hand accounts of the dance-hall girls, entertainers and prostitutes were written or survive today; however, copies of Dawson City's first newspaper, the *Klondike Nugget*, still exist. Stories from its pages tell us much about the Klondike's Paradise Alley. Many of these reports are collected in Jay Moynahan's *Red Light Revelations*. Tales of the habitués of the "wrong side of town" are also related in *High Jinks on the Klondike*, by Richard O'Connor. Lael Morgan's *Good Time Girls* offers an exhaustively researched study of entertainers and prostitutes in the Yukon and Alaska.

About the Author

Author and freelance journalist Rich Mole has been a broadcaster, communications consultant and the president of a successful Vancouver Island advertising agency.

Rich is the author of numerous Klondike books, including *Murder and Mystery in the Yukon* and *Gold Fever: Incredible Tales of the Klondike Gold Rush*. Other non-fiction titles include *Christmas in British Columbia*, *Christmas in the Prairies* and the hockey histories *Great Stanley Cup Victories* and *Against All Odds*, the story of the Edmonton Oilers.

Rich now lives in Calgary, where he is currently at work on a second novel. He can be reached at ramole@telus.net.